ACKNOWLEDGMENTS

My grateful appreciation is extended to

Q. David Bowers
Jerry Cohen
Abner Kreisberg

for their permission to photograph certain coins from their stock. My thanks also to John Murbach and my wife-secretary, Nancy, for their help in preparing this book.

PHOTOGRADE

A PHOTOGRAPHIC GRADING
GUIDE FOR UNITED STATES COINS

BY JAMES F. RUDDY

Life Member American Numismatic Association

All photographs by the author

Published by RUDDY INVESTMENTS

6922 Hollywood Boulevard, Hollywood, Cal. 90028

TO NANCY

Her help and inspiration
cannot be graded highly enough

FOREWORD

Grading is one of the most important and, at the same time, one of the most controversial, areas of numismatics. The difference between, say, Very Fine and Extremely Fine can make a large difference in value. Thus, in the rare coin marketplace grading information plays a leading role.

In the field of numismatic research grading is likewise useful. Common grading terminology permits the interchange of information in a concise manner. Writing about a rare variety of half cent a scholar may note, "The finest specimen known to me grades Very Good." Another student, perhaps thousands of miles away, will then know he has a truly significant and perhaps very valuable piece should he encounter an Extremely Fine or other superior grade coin.

In the present volume James F. Ruddy draws upon his long experience as a coin dealer and as a collector to provide a wealth of information not hitherto available in print. Importantly, the author bases his grading system on the individual coins themselves. For the first time in any grading book such disparate coins as half dimes and dollars are graded by different standards, not by the same criteria.

It should be immediately obvious that if wear on the letters in the word LIBERTY are used as a grading focal point, then a coin with LIBERTY in relief (raised letters)—the U.S. twenty cent piece is an example—should be graded differently from a coin with LIBERTY incused (in sunken letters)—a Liberty seated half dime, for instance. Many early United States coins, particularly those struck during the first decade of the Mint's operations beginning in 1793, were made from hand-cut dies and were struck by methods far different from those in effect after steam presses were installed in 1836. Accordingly, these differences in striking methods must be recognized. A grading system applicable to a one cent piece of 1795 simply cannot be extended to include those of 1855 as well! As the reader will perceive as soon as he uses this book, Mr. Ruddy knows and understands minting and minting procedures and imparts his knowledge to what he writes. In addition, Mr. Ruddy has painstakingly illustrated both the obverse and reverse of each coin. This feature which up to now has not been available is vitally important to the proper grading of a coin. The reader is the benefactor.

I am confident that this volume will be enthusiastically received by those on the buying or selling side of a commercial transaction.

Q. DAVID BOWERS

INTRODUCTION

People have been collecting coins for over 2000 years making it one of the oldest hobbies in the world. Before the twentieth century most collectors categorized their coins as being either new or used. Rarely did the price of a coin dictate that a finer distinction in grading be made. Most often coins could be purchased for a small premium over their face value. The story today is much different. Since the numismatic boom began in the mid 1950's there has been an ever increasing demand for rare coins. The supply is constant since the mintage of a year can never be changed. The natural result was price appreciation. It became increasingly more important to grade coins carefully. Where a difference between Good and Fine meant a dollar or two in the 1950's it might have meant $25 to $50 in the 1960's and possibly will mean $50 to $100 in the 1970's.

The numismatic industry of the 1950's fully realized the need to provide pricing and grading guides that would keep the collector well informed. Many new pricing catalogs were offered on the market and the "Guide Book," long the standard pricing reference, was expanded and continuously being improved. A new weekly newspaper called "Coin World" which featured a regular "Trends of U. S. Coins" section gave collectors week by week price changes. Another weekly newspaper "Numismatic News" now offers a "Tele-Quotes" pricing guide. However in the field of coin grading much less progress has been made. In 1958 Messrs. Brown and Dunn pioneered the standardization of grading by issuing a book which used line drawings to illustrate degrees of wear on a coin. A number of attempts to create standard grading reference works by using photographs of the actual coins were made. Unfortunately the photographic reproduction, and in a few cases, the grading information was inadequate to warrant the acceptance of any of these works as a standard.

Therefore today we are faced with the paradox of excellent progress in pricing information but very little that is new in grading guidelines since 1958. They both are equally important as the value of a coin depends not only on its date and mint mark but on its condition. For example, if you are contemplating buying or selling an 1877 Indian cent which you believe to be in Very Fine condition, you know that the catalog value is $265.00. If you don't know how to grade correctly you may end up buying one which is Fine that catalogs $180.00 or selling one which is really Extremely Fine that catalogs $425.00. Surely this illustrates the need for all collectors and dealers to have an accurate modern pictorial grading guide.

Two years ago after carefully considering the problems involved, I decided to write a book that would fill this need. I knew that four important factors were necessary to produce a successful photographic grading guide. First was the access to between $200,000.00 to $300,000.00 worth of coins needed for photography. I actually ended up taking pictures of coins worth $300,000.00 with close to half of this value pictured in this book. For two years I systematically took pictures of every coin that came through my hands which best represented the average of its grade for its type. I naturally needed help in the more difficult series and asked my good friend, Dave Bowers (we were partners at Empire Coin Company of New York) if I could photograph some coins from his stock. When I told him about this project he enthusiastically offered his help. Jerry Cohen and Abner Kreisberg were very helpful in allowing me to photograph gold coins from their fine stock. Jan Bronson also came to my rescue with a few needed coins. (It might interest you to know that generally speaking the most difficult series of coins to locate were the Small Eagle reverse coins of 1796 and 1797).

Next came research. Fortunately I have had sixteen years of professional coin dealing experience to draw from. In this time I have graded over ten million dollars worth of coins. My schooling and professional training was originally in scientific research. This background taught me to be precise and methodical on very minute details which is vitally important when formalizing a universal grading system.

Photography was by far the most formidable feature to master. The main problem was the extremes involved; the wide range of detail from About Good to About Uncirculated; the size differential from silver three cent pieces to silver dollars; the variations from a dark porous copper surface to a brilliant shiny silver or gold one. Again, I was fortunate to have a background which was of immeasurable help. Before coins became my career I worked in the Physics Research Laboratory of Ansco Film Company where I performed research on all types of photographic film. Even with this experience it took weeks of research to match the right camera, film and light meter to produce the desired results. The camera I chose was an Exacta with a 50mm f1.9 lens and a through-the-lens light metering system. The film was picked for its extreme high resolution, high contrast and fine grain features. Lighting was of paramount importance. Hundreds of test exposures utilizing dozens of various lighting conditions were tried before the first coin picture was taken. Experiments in film processing, background color and the size of the printed coin picture were also necessary. I took over 5,000 photographs to achieve the end result. In many instances a single exposure produced the perfect representation of a certain grade of that type. In other cases it took as many as 20 pictures to produce a single satisfactory one. There are over 1000 different pictures in this book, many more than any other grading book.

Last, but not least, was printing. The firm of Anderson, Ritchie & Simon of Los Angeles was selected because of their outstanding reputation in the field of book printing for over 30 years. An impressive number of their over 1000 titles have won printing awards. We have spared no expense to give you the highest quality printing which reproduces faithfully the original coin photographs. All pictures are printed in fine line screen which produces much finer detail than practically any other coin book of any type in the United States. We used the highest quality 60 pound coated paper which would produce the best results. To top it off we bound the book in a cover with a Marcote coating which is washable and extremely durable.

HOW TO USE THIS GRADING BOOK

Every major type of United States coin is represented in this book. A wide range of conditions are pictured and described. It's easy to check any coin with the uniform arrangement of pictures and descriptions. Simply follow the pictures with your coin until you come to the closest match then check the description beside that picture. Do the same for both the obverse and reverse. The terminology used to describe each condition is in the most basic, concise form for quick reference. General descriptions are as follows:

ABOUT GOOD (AG) represents a very well worn coin which can still be identified as to date and mint. (Note: Coins in Fair condition generally are identifiable only as to type).

GOOD (G) usually indicates an over-all clean appearing coin with all lettering visible and basic features outlined except on coins in the 1700's and early 1800's.

VERY GOOD (VG) is probably one of the easiest grades to describe. In the majority of cases the word "LIBERTY" on the headband or shield can be used to determine this grade. When it is stated that a total of any three letters of "LIBERTY" verify this grade it is taking into consideration the many diverse designs used on all our coins. In some cases three full letters may be visible, in other instances two full and two partial or even one full and four partial letters will show. Of course it is important that all other features of both the obverse and reverse verify this grade.

7

FINE (F) condition is probably the most widely collected circulated condition. All of the major design is usually visible. The word "LIBERTY" (except on twenty cent pieces and Liberty Seated dollars) is complete.

VERY FINE (VF) Some of the more intricate designs will be noticeable. A careful eye is needed to distinguish the differences between this grade and the next.

EXTREMELY FINE (EF or XF). Practically all details will be clearly visible.

ABOUT UNCIRCULATED (AU). A coin that has seen a slight amount of circulation. Often some mint luster will show in the field.

UNCIRCULATED COINS. Since an Uncirculated coin should have no wear it would be difficult to show the absence of wear in a photograph. In order to use this book to check a coin you believe to be Uncirculated compare it with the About Uncirculated photograph and description. It should not show any of the traces of wear that are described. There are variations of the Uncirculated grade. Besides Brilliant Uncirculated (BU) and Toned Uncirculated which are self explanatory, there is Choice Uncirculated and Gem Uncirculated. Choice describes an above average Uncirculated specimen, well struck with a minimum of minor bag marks or minting defects. Gem is the finest obtainable, sharply struck and free of the usual minor bag marks or minting defects. Another variation is Brilliant Uncirculated, light rubbing. This is not an About Uncirculated coin which has seen circulation. Rather it is a strictly Uncirculated coin with full mint luster which may show envelope or cabinet friction or possibly rubbing from an album slide.

PROOF COINS. A coin in Proof condition should have no wear, friction or rubbing of any kind unless it is impaired and so noted. Occasionally the mirror-like surfaces will show minor hairlines usually caused by being rubbed with a cloth during a cleaning operation. These hairlines usually can only be seen with a magnifying glass but should be described as they reduce the value of a Proof coin 10 to 20%. A Matte Proof copper or nickel coin must have a square edge plus a matte finish, not merely a matte-like appearance. The edge must look like this drawing around the entire circumference of the coin.

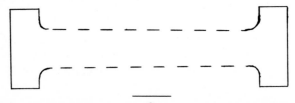

COLOR. An early copper coin showing original mint color is rare and should command a substantial premium. Recently some unscrupulous people have devised a method of cleaning and toning copper coins to give them an artificial but deceiving look of color. There is no way to accurately describe the varied results of this process. Your best protection is to deal only with a reputable dealer. A note of caution: be wary of "bargain" priced early copper coins described as Brilliant Uncirculated or BU. These "bargains" usually cost you, not save you money.

Generally speaking, imperfections such as scratches, dents, edge bumps and light corrosion will lower the condition of a coin by a full grade. Severe imperfections will further reduce its grade.

SPLIT GRADES are often advertised in order to more accurately describe a coin. A coin described as Good to Very Good (G-VG) may show evidence of a letter or two of "LIBERTY" (if that is the diagnostic grading feature) but not the total of three letters necessary to call it Very Good. A coin may have a Fine obverse but only a Very Good reverse and should be described as such. The more valuable a coin the more reason to use split grades as the difference in a half a grade may mean a variation of 10 to 20% of the price. An important consideration for both the buyer and seller.

INTERESTING VARIATIONS

Interesting peculiarities and abnormalities that often appear on coins are pictorially illustrated below. Only a representative sampling can be shown as there are literally thousands of variations in the United States field.

DIE BREAKS. A die break is a raised protrusion on a coin caused when a die that has been broken (usually due to use) is used to strike that coin. Under minting pressure the coin metal is forced into the break in the die. A great number of astute collectors who collect by die varieties eagerly look for such die breaks for quick identification of the variety.

OVERDATES. Probably the most sought after and desirable group of coins in the United States series. If a die was unused or still in excellent condition at the end of a certain minting year the mint would occasionally repunch the date with the next minting year's date causing an overdate. There are over 70 different overdates in the United States field of which about 20 sell for over $1000.00 each and five for over $5000.00 each. A few of the rare and unusual ones are pictured here.

1798/7	1806/4	1888/7	1824/1	1823/2
$10	$2.50	1¢	$2.50	25¢

RE-ENGRAVED DATES. Not to be confused with overdates, re-engraved dates are caused when the die is repunched with the same date. This is ordinarily done to better reposition or strengthen the date.

1795 50¢   1877-CC 25¢

ADJUSTMENT MARKS. In the very early days the crude minting facilities often produced coins weighing too much. Those were frugal times and it was worth while to weigh every silver coin. If it was overweight they would scrape a file over the obverse and/or reverse to take away the required amount of silver. These file marks are called adjustment marks. Since they are of mint origin they should not detract from the monetary value of a coin.

INCUSATION OR CLASH MARKS. This interesting effect can be found on coins of all metals from 1793 to date. They are caused when the obverse and reverse dies come together without a coin planchet between them. The result is that some of the obverse design is permanently inscribed on the reverse die and vice versa. Thereafter every coin minted from these dies exhibits clash marks which should not reduce their value.

COUNTERFEIT COINS. As in any field where money can be made from forgeries or counterfeits, i.e. art, rare stamps, manuscripts and even stock certificates, coins are no exception. Fortunately stringent laws against counterfeiting United States coins keep the abuse to a minimum.

A few simple precautions will usually prevent the collector from being fooled by fake coins. Examine any suspicious coin carefully with a magnifying glass. If there are any tiny raised bubbles or raised rough areas this may indicate a cast or electrotype fake. If a suspicious coin has a non-reeded edge, inspect it for a fine line or seam running all the way around the coin. If such a seam exists the chances are good that the coin is an electrotype.

The simplest and most common method of testing a coin is to "ring it." Balance the test coin on the tip of your index finger, hold it about six inches from your ear and tap the edge very lightly with another coin (pocket change will do). If the coin does not have a bell-like ring there is a good possibility that it is a fake and further testing is recommended. If it does ring it does not guarantee that it is genuine but will eliminate the possibility of its being a crude cast or electrotype, the most common types of counterfeits. Always do your "ring" test over a rug or other safe area in case the coin drops. Try this method with some modern change for practice. Again, I must emphasize that your best protection against fakes is a reputable dealer.

CLEANING. The subject of cleaning should be directed only to nickel, silver and gold coins in top conditions. To clean any of the above mentioned coins in less than About Uncirculated condition will produce an unnatural appearance that is generally not acceptable to most collectors. The cleaning of copper coins in any condition should be avoided unless it is necessary to remove an unsightly fingerprint or large carbon spots.

Use only a clear liquid "dip," not a paste, powder or polish. Pour some dip, full strength, into a pliable plastic dish. Completely immerse the coin in the liquid. Do not leave the coin in the liquid longer than a few seconds. Immediately rinse the coin thoroughly under running cold water. Pat (do not rub) the coin dry with a soft absorbent cloth, a terrycloth towel is recommended. Holding the coin in your fingers and using a cotton swab may result in uneven cleaning. For copper coins use a mixture of half "dip" and half cold water. Always make sure your coins are thoroughly dry and at room temperature before storing. Practice cleaning processes with low value coins.

It is sometimes desirable on circulated coins to remove the light film of oxidation that sometimes forms on copper. A gentle rub with a soft cloth lightly treated with a liquid product called "CARE" will usually accomplish this task. Tape and most glues will come off with an application of acetone which is available at drugstores.

IMPORTANT: The pictures in this book were chosen to represent the average of a particular grade of a type. Naturally variations in variety or strike must be taken into consideration especially in coins minted before 1836. The reader must average out the plus and minus factors when comparing a coin to the average picture. If any early large cent, for example, shows weak letters on the left side and very strong letters on the right, it must be assumed that the coin could not have been worn only on one portion of its surface. Examples such as this result from an improper strike or an uneven planchet. Take into consideration all of the features of each side not just an isolated weak spot which was not a result of wear.

THE AMERICAN NUMISMATIC ASSOCIATION

The American Numismatic Association (A.N.A.) an educational, non-profit organization was founded in 1891. It is the most important numismatic association for a coin collector to join.

Among the many benefits of belonging to the A.N.A. is the highly informative monthly publication "The Numismatist" sent to all members.

For further information about joining the A.N.A. write to their headquarters, P. O. Box 2366, Colorado Springs, Colo. 80901.

COLONIAL   COINS

I have separated the various styles and qualities of strikes among Colonial coins into three basic groups.

The Connecticut cents pictured below represent the first group. These crudely struck pieces were made from hand-crafted dies which often resulted in interesting errors and off-center strikes. Planchet imperfections are quite common in this group. Many people find collecting these different varieties fascinating.

The other popular colonials in this group are: all Massachusetts silver, Mark Newby pieces, Nova Eborac, Auctori Plebis, Voce Populi and Vermont cents.

| GOOD | VG | FINE | VF |

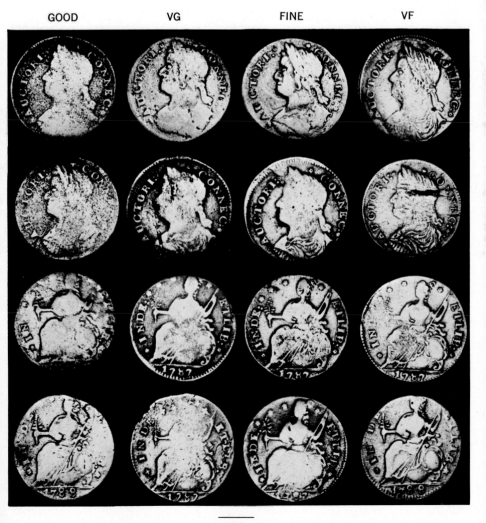

COLONIAL   COINS

I have picked New Jersey cents to represent the middle group or average strikes of the Colonial field.

This group includes Maryland, Rosa Americana, Wood's pieces, New York pieces, Massachusetts copper coins, Continental dollars, Nova Constellatio cents, French Colonies, Chalmers, Elephant tokens, Virginia halfpennies, North American tokens, Pitt tokens, Washington pieces of United States origin and Fugio cents.

| GOOD | VG | FINE | VF |

COLONIAL   COINS

For the well struck group I use the Washington pieces of English origin to illustrate the quality of striking.

Also in this group are the Bar cents, Talbot Allum & Lee cents, Kentucky tokens, Myddelton tokens, Franklin Press cents and the Rhode Island Ship tokens.

NOTE: These coins are rarely found in less than very good condition.

VG	FINE	VF	EF

ABOUT GOOD
Head and wreath will be distinct, a partial date must show. "LIBERTY" may not be distinct.

GOOD
Most of the lettering and design will be readable. The outline of the head will stand out boldly.

VERY GOOD
Some hair detail will be visible. Date will be bold.

FINE
About one-third of the hair detail will show. All of the lettering will be clear.

VERY FINE
At least half of the hair detail will be sharp. The hair ribbon will be distinct.

ABOUT GOOD

The wreath will be almost complete but only a few letters of the legend will be readable.

GOOD

The wreath will be complete. Half of the legend will be readable.

VERY GOOD

The legend will be complete but some letters will be weak.

Note: The words "HALF CENT" were struck weakly on certain varieties and should not be used to determine condition.

FINE

The leaves and berries in the wreath although complete will be quite flat.

VERY FINE

The leaves in the wreath will be stronger but will not show leaf detail.

EXTREMELY FINE

All major hair detail will show but be worn on the high spots at the shoulder and to the right of the ear.

ABOUT UNCIRCULATED

Only a trace of wear will show on Liberty's cheek and the hair to the right of her ear.

LIBERTY CAP HALF CENTS 1794-1797

ABOUT GOOD

The head will be outlined but worn smooth. Lettering will be worn with a partial date showing.

GOOD

Most of "LIBERTY" will show. The date will be readable but may be quite weak.

VERY GOOD

Some hair detail will show by the shoulder. "LIBERTY" will be strong but the date still may be weak depending on the variety.

EXTREMELY FINE

The leaves in the wreath will show some detail and appear more rounded.

ABOUT UNCIRCULATED

Most leaves will show full detail although some may not be fully struck up.

LIBERTY CAP HALF CENTS 1794-1797

ABOUT GOOD

A partial wreath and legend will show but be very weak.

Note: The words "HALF CENT" were struck weakly on certain varieties and should not be used to determine condition.

GOOD

The wreath will be quite weak but should be complete. At least half of the legend will be readable.

VERY GOOD

The wreath will be complete. The legend will be complete except on die varieties which were always weakly struck.

FINE
About one-third of Liberty's hair will show plainly. The date will be clearly defined.

VERY FINE
At least half of Liberty's hair will be distinct. *Note:* If a coin shows weakness on only one section of the obverse or reverse it is probably due to the design and striking of that particular variety. This should be disregarded when determining condition.

EXTREMELY FINE
Almost full hair detail on Liberty's head but definite wear will show around the ear and neck.

ABOUT UNCIRCULATED
Wear will show only on the highest waves of hair around the ear and neck.

DRAPED BUST HALF CENTS 1800-1808

ABOUT GOOD
An outline of the head and a partial date will show.

FINE

The wreath will be bold but worn flat. There will not be any leaf detail.

VERY FINE

About half of the leaves will be individually separated but still show no detail.

EXTREMELY FINE

All of the leaves will be separated from each other. There will be some leaf detail on the bottom leaves.

ABOUT UNCIRCULATED

Most of the leaves will show full detail and will be worn on the highest points only.

DRAPED BUST HALF CENTS 1800-1808

ABOUT GOOD

A partial wreath and legend will show.

GOOD

The head will be sharply outlined. All lettering will be readable although weak.

VERY GOOD

Hair detail will begin to show at the shoulder. "LIBERTY" will be strong.

FINE

Drapery on the bust will show but be worn at the top. About one-half of the hair detail will be visible.

Note: The bulge over the letters "RTY" is caused by a die break. Die breaks do not alter the condition of a coin.

VERY FINE

About two-thirds of the hair detail will be visible. The top line of drapery will be complete to the hair.

EXTREMELY FINE

All hair detail will show but will be weak above the forehead and ear. Drapery will be well defined.

GOOD

The wreath will be complete. There may be wear on the tops of some of the letters of the legend.

VERY GOOD

The lettering will be complete. Wreath will be bold but worn flat.

FINE

A few leaves will be separated and show some detail.

VERY FINE

Almost all of the leaves will be separated. The bottom leaves will show some detail.

EXTREMELY FINE

Most of the leaves will show detail.

ABOUT UNCIRCULATED

There will be slight wear on hair above the fore-head and to the left of the ear.

TURBAN HEAD HALF CENTS 1809-1836

ABOUT GOOD

The rim will be worn down to the stars and date. Some "LIBERTY" may show.

GOOD

The head will be well outlined and may show a full "LIBERTY." Date will be bold.

VERY GOOD

Hair detail and the ear will begin to show. There must be a full "LIBERTY."

FINE

Two-thirds of the hair detail will show. Hair curl on neck will show clearly although hair above the forehead will be worn. "LIBERTY" will be strong.

ABOUT UNCIRCULATED

There will be only a trace of wear on the highest points of the leaves.

TURBAN HEAD HALF CENTS 1809-1836

ABOUT GOOD

Only a partial legend will show. "HALF CENT" will be readable.

GOOD

The rim will be worn down to the tops of the letters but all lettering will be readable.

VERY GOOD

All letters will be complete. The wreath will be bold but worn almost flat.

FINE

Most of the leaves will be separated, a few will show detail.

VERY FINE

All hair will show but will be weak around Liberty's face and below ear.

EXTREMELY FINE

Full hair will show but there will be wear on the highest points.

ABOUT UNCIRCULATED

The hair detail will be very sharp with only a trace of wear on the highest points.

HALF CENT TOKEN 1837

FINE

There will only be a trace of detail on the eagle's wings.

Note: Rarely found in conditions below Fine.

VERY FINE

About two-thirds of the eagle's wings will show feathers.

VERY FINE

Approximately half of the leaves will show detail and all will be separated.

EXTREMELY FINE

All of the leaves will show some detail.

ABOUT UNCIRCULATED

Slight wear will show on only the highest points of the top leaves.

HALF CENT TOKEN 1837

FINE

The leaves in the wreath will be separated and a few will show detail.

VERY FINE

About half of the leaves will show detail.

EXTREMELY FINE

All of the eagle's feathers will show but will be worn on the high points.

ABOUT UNCIRCULATED

There will be a trace of wear only on the highest points of the feathers. The top of the eagle's right wing may be flatly struck.

BRAIDED HAIR HALF CENTS 1840-1857

VERY GOOD

Full "LIBERTY" but "L" will be weak. About half of the hair detail will be visible but not sharp.

Note: Rarely found in conditions below Very Good.

FINE

Hair cord will be sharp. Hair around the face will be outlined but worn.

VERY FINE

All hair detail will show but will be weak above the ear and by the neck.

EXTREMELY FINE
More detail will show on the leaves.

ABOUT UNCIRCULATED
Slight wear will be visible on only the highest points of the leaves.

BRAIDED HAIR HALF CENTS 1840-1857

VERY GOOD
The wreath will be outlined with the leaves worn flat.

FINE
Most leaves will be separated and begin to show some detail.

VERY FINE
About half of the leaves will show detail.

EXTREMELY FINE

All hair detail will be well outlined with wear only on the highest points.

ABOUT UNCIRCULATED

Only the slightest trace of wear will show on Liberty's hair above her ear.

1793 CHAIN LARGE CENT

FAIR

Identifiable as to type by the distinct head type. No date will show.

ABOUT GOOD

The head will be well worn. A partial date must show.

GOOD

The head will be outlined although worn flat. The date will show but may be worn at the bottom or weakly struck.

ABOUT GOOD

Most of the wreath will be clear with only a few letters visible.

GOOD

The rim may be worn down into some of the letters.

VERY GOOD

All of the lettering will be clear.
Note: Some of the letters may be weak due to striking.

FINE

The wreath will be well outlined but flat. Lettering will be sharp.

VERY FINE

The beaded border will be sharp. Leaves will be separated but worn flat.

EXTREMELY FINE

There will be wear on the highest points of hair from the forehead to the shoulder.

ABOUT UNCIRCULATED

The hair detail will be complete but worn on the highest points to the left of the ear and neck.

LIBERTY CAP LARGE CENTS 1793-1796

ABOUT GOOD

The head and some lettering will be visible. Date will be readable although weak.

GOOD

The head will be well outlined. Most of the lettering and date will be clearly readable.

VERY GOOD

Some hair detail will show. All lettering will be distinct.

Note: There may be weakness in spots due to the methods of striking these early coins.

EXTREMELY FINE
There will be a slight roundness to the leaves.

ABOUT UNCIRCULATED
The leaves will be well rounded with wear only on the highest points.

LIBERTY CAP LARGE CENTS 1793-1796

ABOUT GOOD
Most of the wreath will be clear with only a few letters visible.

GOOD
The rim may be worn down into some of the letters which will be visible but weak.

Note: The words "ONE CENT" were struck weakly on certain varieties and should not be used to determine condition.

VERY GOOD
All of the lettering will be clear.

FINE
Approximately one-half of Liberty's hair will show clearly.

VERY FINE
The hair behind Liberty's ear and above her forehead will be worn but the rest of the hair will be detailed.

EXTREMELY FINE
All major hair detail will be visible with wear only on high spots.

ABOUT UNCIRCULATED
All of the hair detail will be strong but will show a trace of wear on the highest points.

DRAPED BUST LARGE CENTS 1796-1807

ABOUT GOOD
The head will be outlined and the date will be readable but weak.

FINE
The wreath will be well outlined but flat.

VERY FINE
The leaves will be separated but show very little detail.

EXTREMELY FINE
The leaves will be well defined with some leaves showing detail.

ABOUT UNCIRCULATED
Leaf detail will be quite distinct with only slight wear visible.

DRAPED BUST LARGE CENTS 1796-1807

ABOUT GOOD
Half of the lettering will be visible.

39

GOOD
The head will be distinctly outlined.

VERY GOOD
About one-third of the hair detail will show. The date will be bold.

FINE
Approximately two-thirds of the hair detail will show. The hair will be smooth above Liberty's forehead, the top of her head and to the left of her neck.

VERY FINE
Almost all of the hair will be visible but will be worn flat at the highest points.

Note: These coins were made over 150 years ago and often were unevenly struck or had imperfections that cannot be standardized in any grading book. These factors must be taken into consideration when grading early coins.

EXTREMELY FINE
Full hair will show but have wear on the tips of the curls and to the right of her forehead.

GOOD

All of the letters will be readable although the rim may be worn down into some of them because of uneven striking.

VERY GOOD

All letters will show. The wreath will be outlined but show no detail.

FINE

Some of the leaves will show individual separation.

VERY FINE

Each individual leaf will be well defined with little detail showing.

EXTREMELY FINE

Most of the leaves will show detail but be worn on all the high points.

ABOUT UNCIRCULATED

All hair detail will be sharp. There will only be a trace of wear on the highest points of hair.

TURBAN HEAD LARGE CENTS 1808-1814

ABOUT GOOD

The rim will be worn down into the stars. Date will be readable but weak.

GOOD

The date and stars will be clear. The head will be distinctly outlined. A partial "LIBERTY" may show.

VERY GOOD

About one-third of the hair detail will show and the ear will be visible. A full "LIBERTY" will show.

FINE

About two-thirds of the hair will show, but weakly. Hair around the face will be worn almost smooth. The ear will be sharp.

42

ABOUT UNCIRCULATED

All of the leaves will show detail or be well rounded. Wear will show only on the very highest points.

TURBAN HEAD LARGE CENTS 1808-1814

ABOUT GOOD

Half of the lettering will be visible.

GOOD

All of the letters will be readable although the rim may be worn down into some of them because of uneven striking.

VERY GOOD

All of the letters will show although some may be weakly struck. The wreath will be flat but well defined.

FINE

The top leaves on the wreath will be worn flat.

43

VERY FINE

All of the hair will show but be quite weak in detail.

EXTREMELY FINE

Full hair will show but be worn above the eye, above "LIBERTY" and on the tips of the curls.

ABOUT UNCIRCULATED

The hair will be quite sharp with only a trace of wear on the highest points.

Note: The hair above the word "LIBERTY" was usually weakly struck.

CORONET TYPE LARGE CENTS 1816-1839

ABOUT GOOD

The rim will be worn down into the stars. The date will be readable but weak.

GOOD

The date and stars will be clear. The head will be distinctly outlined. A partial "LIBERTY" may show.

VERY FINE
The top leaves and bow will show some detail.

EXTREMELY FINE
The high points of the leaves will show wear.

ABOUT UNCIRCULATED
There will be only a trace of wear on the highest points of the leaves and wreath bow.

CORONET TYPE LARGE CENTS 1816-1839

ABOUT GOOD
Half of the lettering will be visible.

GOOD
All of the letters will be readable although the rim may be worn down into some of them because of uneven striking.

VERY GOOD

About one-third of the hair detail will be visible. The hair cords will begin to show. "LIBERTY" will be full.

FINE

Most of the major hair detail will be visible. The hair cords will show weakly.

VERY FINE

The hair will be worn flat on the highest points. Both hair cords will show plainly.

EXTREMELY FINE

The hair will be sharp with weakness showing only above the forehead and at the highest point on top of the head. Hair cords will stand out sharply.

ABOUT UNCIRCULATED

Only a trace of wear will be visible on the highest points of the hair.

VERY GOOD

All of the letters will show strongly. The wreath will be flat but well defined.

FINE

The top leaves and the wreath bow will be worn flat.

VERY FINE

The top leaves and bow will show some detail.

EXTREMELY FINE

The highest points of the leaves will show wear.

ABOUT UNCIRCULATED

There will be a trace of wear only on the highest points of the leaves and wreath bow.

ABOUT GOOD

The date and stars will be weak but visible.

GOOD

The date and stars will be clear. The head will be distinctly outlined. A partial "LIBERTY" may show.

VERY GOOD

"LIBERTY" will be readable but "L" and "I" will be weak. About one-third of the hair detail will be clear.

FINE

Approximately two-thirds of the hair will show. Hair above the eye will show but be worn. Beaded hair cords will be sharp.

VERY FINE

All hairlines will be complete but some will be weak especially on top of the head. Hair above the eye and the beaded hair cords will be well defined.

BRAIDED HAIR LARGE CENTS 1840-1857

ABOUT GOOD
Half of the lettering will be visible.

GOOD
All of the lettering will be readable although the rim may be worn down to the tops of some of the letters.

VERY GOOD
All of the lettering will show strongly. The wreath will be flat but well defined.

FINE
The top leaves will be worn flat.

VERY FINE
The top leaves will show some detail.

EXTREMELY FINE
The hair above the ear will be slightly worn.

ABOUT UNCIRCULATED
Only a trace of wear will show on the highest points of the hair above the ear and eye.

FLYING EAGLE CENTS 1856-1858

ABOUT GOOD
The date will be weak but readable.

GOOD
The lettering and date will be readable although the rim may be worn down to the tops of the letters.

VERY GOOD
About one-third of the feathers on the eagle will show but will be weak.

EXTREMELY FINE
The highest points of the leaves will show wear.

ABOUT UNCIRCULATED
There will be a trace of wear only on the highest points of the leaves and wreath bow.

FLYING EAGLE CENTS 1856-1858

ABOUT GOOD
The rim will be worn down into the wreath.

GOOD
The wreath will be completely outlined but worn flat.

VERY GOOD
The wreath will show some detail but be worn smooth on top.

51

FINE

Approximately half of the feathers on the eagle will show. The detail of the eagle's head will be very clear.

VERY FINE

Three-quarters of the feathers will show sharply. The eagle's tail feathers will be complete. There will be considerable flatness on the eagle's breast.

EXTREMELY FINE

There will be wear on the eagle's breast and left wing tip. All other details will be sharp.

ABOUT UNCIRCULATED

There will be only a trace of wear on the eagle's breast and left wing tip.

Note: Weakness of lettering and date may appear on some 1857 cents due to poor striking.

INDIAN HEAD CENTS 1859-1909

ABOUT GOOD

The rim will be worn down well into the letters. The date will be weak but readable.

FINE

More detail will appear on the wreath.

VERY FINE

The ends of the leaves will be worn smooth.
Note: The words "ONE CENT" are sometimes weak due to striking.

EXTREMELY FINE

There will be wear on the high points of the leaves and ribbon bow.

ABOUT UNCIRCULATED

Only a trace of wear will show on the highest points of the leaves and bow.

INDIAN HEAD CENTS 1859-1909

ABOUT GOOD

The rim will be worn down into the wreath.

GOOD

The outline of the Indian will be distinct. "LIB-ERTY" will not show on the headband. The rim may be worn down to the tops of the letters.

VERY GOOD

A total of any three letters of "LIBERTY" will show. This could be a combination of two full letters plus two half letters as not all dates of Indian cents wore uniformly.

FINE

A full "LIBERTY" will be visible but it will not be sharp.

VERY FINE

A full sharp "LIBERTY" will be visible even though there is some wear. The feathers will be worn on the tips.

Note: Indian cents cannot be graded by the diamond designs on the ribbon as this feature was not always sharply struck even in un-circulated grades.

EXTREMELY FINE

There must be a full sharp "LIBERTY." The ends of the feathers will be sharply detailed.

54

GOOD

The wreath will be completely outlined but worn flat.

VERY GOOD

The wreath will begin to show some detail.
Note: The bottom of the "N" in "ONE" may be weak due to striking.

FINE

The top part of the leaves will be worn smooth. The ribbon bow will show considerable wear.

VERY FINE

There will be more detail in the leaves and ribbon bow.

EXTREMELY FINE

There will be wear on the high points of the leaves and ribbon bow.

ABOUT UNCIRCULATED

Only a trace of wear will show on the highest points such as above the ear and the lowest curl of hair.

LINCOLN HEAD CENTS 1909 to date

ABOUT GOOD

The rim will be worn down into the letters. Date and mintmark will be weak but readable.

GOOD

Letters in the legend may be touching the rim. The date will be full.

VERY GOOD

All letters in the legend will be sharp and clear. A few hair details will begin to show.

FINE

Lincoln's ear and bow tie will be clearly visible.

ABOUT UNCIRCULATED

Only a trace of wear will show on the highest points of the leaves and ribbon bow.

LINCOLN HEAD CENTS 1909 -1958

ABOUT GOOD

The rim will be worn down into the letters and the wheat stalks.

GOOD

The wheat stalks will be worn smooth but distinctly outlined.

VERY GOOD

About half of the lines in the upper wheat stalks will show.

FINE

The parallel lines in the upper wheat stalks will show plainly and be separated even though worn. One side or the other may show a weak area at the top of the stalk.

VERY FINE

The ear and bow tie will be sharp. All of Lincoln's hair will be visible but worn. The cheek and jaw details on Lincoln's face will show clearly.

EXTREMELY FINE

There will be wear only on the high points of Lincoln's head and face.

ABOUT UNCIRCULATED

Only the slightest trace of wear will show on the high points of Lincoln's cheek and jaw.

TWO CENT PIECES 1864-1873

ABOUT GOOD

The rim will be worn down into the date and wreath.

GOOD

The date will be clear. A partial "IN GOD WE TRUST" must show.

VERY FINE

The lines in the wheat stalks will be full and show no weak spots.

EXTREMELY FINE

The lines in the wheat stalks will be very bold and clearly defined.

ABOUT UNCIRCULATED

Only a trace of wear will show on the wheat stalks.

TWO CENT PIECES 1864-1873

ABOUT GOOD

Half of the lettering will be visible.

GOOD

All of the lettering will be visible although a few letters may be weak.

VERY GOOD

The motto "IN GOD" and "TRUST" will show clearly. There will be a slight trace of the word "WE."

FINE

The motto "IN GOD WE TRUST" will show completely but the "WE" will be quite weak.

VERY FINE

The entire motto will be readable including the "WE."

Note: The horizontal lines in the shield may not be complete even on higher grade coins due to striking.

EXTREMELY FINE

The full motto will be boldly readable. The leaves will show considerable detail especially at the bottom.

ABOUT UNCIRCULATED

There will be only a trace of wear on the highest points of the design such as the tips of the leaves, the arrow points and the word "WE."

VERY GOOD
All of the lettering will be bold. Half of the wheat grains will show.

FINE
Almost all of the wheat grains will show.

VERY FINE
All of the wheat grains will show plainly.

EXTREMELY FINE
The high points of the wreath and ribbon will show wear.

ABOUT UNCIRCULATED
There will be a trace of wear only on the highest points of the wreath and ribbon.

NICKEL THREE CENT PIECES 1865-1889

ABOUT GOOD

The rim will be worn down into some of the letters.

GOOD

The rim will be worn down to the tops of the letters.

VERY GOOD

There will be a full rim. Very little hair detail will show.

FINE

About one-third of the hair detail will show. *Note:* This coin usually comes with weak hair detail over the ear even on higher grade coins.

VERY FINE

Two-thirds of the hair detail will show plainly.

ABOUT GOOD
The rim will be worn down into the wreath.

GOOD
The leaves in the wreath will be flat and only a few will be separated.

VERY GOOD
There will be a full rim. About half of the leaves will be separated from each other.

FINE
All of the leaves will be separated. Some of the lines will show weakly in the Roman numeral III.

VERY FINE
The lines will be sharper.

Note: This coin often comes with weakly struck lines even on higher grade coins.

EXTREMELY FINE

The upper hair and lower curls should be very sharp.

ABOUT UNCIRCULATED

Only the slightest trace of wear will show on the hair curls and the hair above the forehead.

SHIELD NICKELS 1866-1883

ABOUT GOOD

The rim will be worn down into the letters and wreath.

GOOD

The date and all letters should be clear although the rim may be worn down to the tops of the letters. Leaves will be flat.

VERY GOOD

The leaves will show slight detail. Some of the horizontal lines in the shield will show.

EXTREMELY FINE

All of the lines will be boldly visible in at least one figure of the Roman numeral. There will be wear only on the tips of the leaves.

ABOUT UNCIRCULATED

Only a trace of wear will show on the wreath and Roman numerals.

SHIELD NICKELS 1866-1883

ABOUT GOOD

The rim will be worn down into the letters.

GOOD

The rim will be worn down to the tops of the letters.

VERY GOOD

There will be a full rim.

Note: The figure "5" may be weak in spots due to striking. This should not affect the grade.

65

FINE

Individual leaves will be separated but worn smooth halfway from the tips to the center of the leaves.

VERY FINE

The leaves will be more defined and clearly separated.

Note: The horizontal lines in the shield may be incomplete because of striking even on higher grades and should not affect the grading.

EXTREMELY FINE

The leaves will stand out in bold relief with most of the center lines showing clearly.

ABOUT UNCIRCULATED

Only a trace of wear will show on the tips of the leaves and on the highest points of the shield.

LIBERTY HEAD NICKELS 1883-1913

ABOUT GOOD

The rim will be worn down into the stars and/or the date.

FINE

The stars, with a few lines showing, will be very bold.

VERY FINE

Most of the lines in the stars will be complete.

Note: If some stars are strong and some weak, determine condition by the strong ones. The weakness is due to striking.

EXTREMELY FINE

The strongest stars will show full sharp lines.

ABOUT UNCIRCULATED

The stars will show only a trace of wear.

LIBERTY HEAD NICKELS 1883-1913

ABOUT GOOD

The figure "V" and the wreath will be visible.

GOOD
Liberty will be outlined boldly but "LIBERTY" will not show on the headband.

VERY GOOD
A total of any three letters of "LIBERTY" must show.

FINE
A full "LIBERTY" must be readable including the letter "I." About 50% of the hair detail will be visible.

VERY FINE
"LIBERTY" will be complete and bold. The hair will show about 75% detail.

EXTREMELY FINE
"LIBERTY" will be very bold. All of the hair details will be visible but may be weak on the high points above the ear and forehead.

GOOD

The rim may be worn down to the tops of the letters. "E PLURIBUS UNUM" will be barely visible.

VERY GOOD

The wreath will be sharply outlined. "E PLU-RIBUS UNUM" will show weakly.

FINE

Detail will begin to appear in the wreath. "E PLURIBUS UNUM" will be strong.

VERY FINE

Partial detail will show on the leaves of the wreath and the ear of corn.

EXTREMELY FINE

There will be wear on the high points of the wreath and ear of corn.

ABOUT UNCIRCULATED

There will be only the slightest trace of wear on the highest portion of hair above the ear and forehead.

BUFFALO NICKELS 1913-1938

ABOUT GOOD

The rim will be worn down well into the letters. Only a partial date will show but enough to be recognizable.

GOOD

The rim will be worn down into the tops of the letters of "LIBERTY." The date will be readable but some of the numbers will be well worn.

VERY GOOD

The rim may touch the tops of the letters of "LIBERTY." The date will be distinct.

FINE

"LIBERTY" will be separated from the rim. The date will be very bold.

ABOUT UNCIRCULATED

There will be only a trace of wear on the highest portions of the wreath.

BUFFALO NICKELS 1913-1938

ABOUT GOOD

The rim is worn down into the letters.

GOOD

The rim may be worn down into the tops of the letters. The horn need not show.

VERY GOOD

There will be a full rim. Half of the horn will show. The buffalo's back will be almost smooth.

FINE

Two-thirds of a horn will show. The major detail on the buffalo's back will show.

71

VERY FINE

The hair braid and cheek will show some detail but be flat on the high spots.

EXTREMELY FINE

The hair braid and face details on the Indian are now very bold with only slight wear on the high points.

ABOUT UNCIRCULATED

There is only the slightest trace of wear on the highest point of the cheek.

Note: Buffalo nickels often come weakly struck which results in a weak horn or tail on the reverse, weak detail and "LIBERTY" on the obverse even on uncirculated specimens.

JEFFERSON NICKELS 1938 to date

GOOD

The rim will be worn down to the tops of the letters. The head will be worn flat.

VERY GOOD

The rim will be worn down to the tops of the letters. Only the hair on the back of the head will show detail.

72

VERY FINE

There will be a full horn but the top may not be well outlined. The hair on the buffalo's head will be well worn.

EXTREMELY FINE

A full sharp horn will show. The tail will show on the hip. Flat spots of wear will show on the head, upper front leg and hip.

ABOUT UNCIRCULATED

There will be only a trace of wear on the highest points of the upper front leg and hip. The tail will be sharp.

JEFFERSON NICKELS 1938 to date

GOOD

Monticello will be worn smooth.

VERY GOOD

The four main pillars will show but be very weak.

73

FINE
Approximately half of the major hair detail will show. The cheek will be worn flat.

VERY FINE
About three-quarters of the major hair detail will show.

EXTREMELY FINE
All of the hair detail will show but will be worn on the high points. The cheekbone will be well rounded but show wear.

ABOUT UNCIRCULATED
There will be a trace of wear on the cheekbone and highest points of the hair.

SILVER THREE CENT PIECES 1851-1873

ABOUT GOOD
Approximately half of the lettering will show.

FINE

The two outer pillars will be well outlined. The two inner pillars will show but may not be complete from top to bottom.

VERY FINE

All four pillars will be well defined. The archway above the pillars will show major detail.

EXTREMELY FINE

All details on Monticello will show except the triangle in the arch above the pillars.

ABOUT UNCIRCULATED

All details on Monticello will be sharp including the triangle. There will be only a trace of wear on the highest points.

Note: The steps on Monticello will be full on only very well struck pieces and should command a premium price.

SILVER THREE CENT PIECES 1851-1873

ABOUT GOOD

The rim will be worn down well into the stars.

GOOD

The rim may be worn down into a few letters and part of the date.

VERY GOOD

The letters and date will be full. The shield in the center of the star may not be fully outlined.

FINE

The shield will be complete.

VERY FINE

The star will be bold but show definite signs of wear on the high points and tips.

EXTREMELY FINE

The star and shield will be very bold.

GOOD
The rim will be worn down to the tops of the stars.

VERY GOOD
The stars will be well outlined and separated from the rim.

FINE
The design in the "C" will begin to show.

VERY FINE
The design in the "C" will be separated inside the circles.

EXTREMELY FINE
The design in the "C" will now be well rounded.

The star will show only a trace of wear on the top of each star point.

Note: The center of the shield may be weak due to striking on some pieces.

FLOWING HAIR HALF DIMES 1794-1795

ABOUT GOOD

The rim will be worn down into the stars, legend and/or date.

GOOD

The bust will be outlined but will not show detail. The date, stars and lettering will be readable.

VERY GOOD

Some detail will show on the ends of the hair. The major facial details will show.

FINE

About half of the major hair detail will show.

ABOUT UNCIRCULATED

Only a trace of wear will appear on the design in the "C" and on the Roman numeral.

FLOWING HAIR HALF DIMES 1794-1795

ABOUT GOOD

The rim will be worn down well into the lettering and design.

GOOD

The rim will be worn into the tops of a few letters. The eagle will be outlined but show no detail.

VERY GOOD

All of the letters will be fully visible. The wings will show a few feather details.

FINE

A few more feathers will show in the wings. The leaves will be worn flat.

VERY FINE

The hair above Liberty's forehead will be outlined and will show major details.

EXTREMELY FINE

All of the hair detail will show. There will be wear only on the high waves of hair.

ABOUT UNCIRCULATED

Only a trace of wear will be visible on the high waves of hair around the face and ear.

Note: There may be weakness due to striking on the hair behind the ear.

DRAPED BUST HALF DIMES 1796-1805

ABOUT GOOD

The rim will be worn down into the stars, "LIBERTY" and/or date. The head will be worn flat.

GOOD

The rim will be worn down to the tops of the stars. A few letters of "LIBERTY" may be worn. Head will be well outlined.

VERY FINE

About half of the feathers will show. The leaves will be rounded but show no detail.

EXTREMELY FINE

Most of the feathers will show in the wings. Partial detail will be visible in the leaves.

ABOUT UNCIRCULATED

Only a trace of wear will appear on the head and top edges of the eagle's wings.

Note: Because of striking the breast rarely comes with full feather detail even on Uncirculated specimens.

DRAPED BUST HALF DIMES 1796-1805

(For 1800-1805 reverses see page 95)

ABOUT GOOD

The rim will be worn down well into the letters and design.

GOOD

The rim will be worn down to the tops of some of the letters. The eagle will be outlined but show no detail.

81

VERY GOOD

About one-quarter of the hair detail will show, mostly in the lower curls. Some evidence of drapery lines will show.

FINE

Approximately half of the hair detail will show.

VERY FINE

About three-quarters of the hair detail will show.

Note: Drapery lines across Liberty's bust cannot be used to determine grade as they vary drastically in detail from coin to coin because of striking.

EXTREMELY FINE

All of the major detail of the hair will show. Wear will be visible to the left of the forehead.

ABOUT UNCIRCULATED

Only a slight trace of wear will be visible on Liberty's bust, shoulder and hair left of her forehead.

Note: Hair may be flat to the left of Liberty's neck due to striking.

VERY GOOD
All of the letters will be fully visible.

FINE
Some feathers will show in the wings.

VERY FINE
About half of the wing feathers will show.

EXTREMELY FINE
Most of the feathers will show in the wings.
Note: The breast feathers are rarely visible because of striking even on high grade specimens.

ABOUT UNCIRCULATED
Only a trace of wear will appear on the head and top edges of the wings.

ABOUT GOOD

The rim will be worn down into the stars and/or date. The head will be worn smooth.

GOOD

The head will be flat. At least half of "LIBERTY" will be readable.

VERY GOOD

There will be a full "LIBERTY." About half of the hair detail will be visible.

FINE

The lower drapery folds will be sharp. About three-quarters of the hair detail will show.

VERY FINE

All of the major details of the hair will show except the curl on the neck. The ear and drapery clasp will show clearly.

CAPPED HALF DIMES 1829-1837

ABOUT GOOD
About half of the lettering will be visible.

GOOD
All of the lettering will be complete. The eagle will be flat. There may not be a full "E PLURIBUS UNUM."

VERY GOOD
"E PLURIBUS UNUM" will be complete. There will be a few feathers showing in the eagle's left wing.

FINE
Approximately half of the feathers will show in the eagle's wings.

VERY FINE
Three-quarters of the feathers will show. The neck and right leg will show considerable wear.

EXTREMELY FINE

All of the hair will be sharp with wear only on the highest curls. The curl on the neck will show.

ABOUT UNCIRCULATED

There will be only a trace of wear on the highest points of the hair above the forehead and ear.

HALF DIMES 1837-1838 (no stars)

ABOUT GOOD

The rim will be worn down into the field and may be worn into the date and/or head.

GOOD

There will be a full outline of Liberty. The shield will be worn smooth.

VERY GOOD

A total of any three letters of "LIBERTY" will be visible on the shield.

EXTREMELY FINE

All of the feathers will show but will be worn on the highest points. The edges of both wings will be worn.

ABOUT UNCIRCULATED

There will be only a trace of wear on the eagle's claws, neck and along the edges of the wings.

Note: The right wing of the eagle and the center of "E PLURIBUS UNUM" may be flat due to striking.

HALF DIMES 1837-1838 (no stars)

ABOUT GOOD

Approximately half of the lettering will be visible.

GOOD

The rim will be worn down to the tops of some of the letters.

VERY GOOD

There will be a full rim. The leaves in the wreath will be outlined but not well defined.

FINE

There will be a full "LIBERTY" on the shield but it will not be sharp.

VERY FINE

"LIBERTY" will be sharp. Only the deepest folds of Liberty's gown will be visible.

EXTREMELY FINE

There will be wear on Liberty's breast and legs.

ABOUT UNCIRCULATED

Only a trace of wear will appear on Liberty's breast and knees.

Note: The horizontal lines of the shield often come weak even on higher grades.

LIBERTY SEATED HALF DIMES 1838-1859

ABOUT GOOD

The rim will be worn down into the date and/or stars.

FINE

The leaves will be separated but little detail will show.

VERY FINE

About half of the leaves will show detail.

EXTREMELY FINE

All of the leaves will show detail but be worn on the ends.

ABOUT UNCIRCULATED

Only a trace of wear will be visible on the ribbon bow and the tips of the leaves.

LIBERTY SEATED HALF DIMES 1838-1859

ABOUT GOOD

About half of the lettering will be visible.

GOOD

There will be a full outline of Liberty. The shield will be worn smooth.

VERY GOOD

A total of any three letters of "LIBERTY" will be visible on the shield.

FINE

There will be a full "LIBERTY" on the shield but it will not be sharp.

VERY FINE

"LIBERTY" will be sharp. Only the deepest folds of Liberty's gown will be visible.

EXTREMELY FINE

There will be wear on Liberty's head, breast and legs.

GOOD

The rim will be worn down to the tops of some of the letters.

VERY GOOD

There will be a full rim. The leaves in the wreath will be outlined but not well defined.

FINE

The leaves will be separated but will have little detail.

VERY FINE

Approximately half of the leaves will show detail.

EXTREMELY FINE

All of the leaves will show detail but be worn on the ends.

ABOUT UNCIRCULATED

Only a trace of wear will appear on Liberty's breast and knees.

Note: The clasp of Liberty's gown may be weak due to striking and therefore cannot be used to determine condition.

LIBERTY SEATED HALF DIMES 1860-1873

ABOUT GOOD

The rim will be worn down into the letters and/or date.

GOOD

There will be a full rim. "LIBERTY" will not show.

VERY GOOD

A total of any three letters of "LIBERTY" will be visible.

FINE

There will be a full "LIBERTY" but it will not be sharp. Only the deepest folds of Liberty's gown will be visible.

ABOUT UNCIRCULATED

Only a trace of wear will be visible on the ribbon bow and the tips of the leaves.

LIBERTY SEATED HALF DIMES 1860-1873

ABOUT GOOD

About half of the letters and/or design will be worn away.

GOOD

There will be a full rim. The wreath will be worn flat.

VERY GOOD

Approximately half of the major detail will show in the wreath.

FINE

All of the major detail will be visible but show definite wear.

VERY FINE

"LIBERTY" will be sharp. More detail will be visible on the upper folds of Liberty's gown.

EXTREMELY FINE

There will be wear on Liberty's head, breast and legs.

ABOUT UNCIRCULATED

Only a trace of wear will appear on Liberty's breast and knees.

DRAPED BUST DIMES 1796-1807

ABOUT GOOD

The rim will be worn down into the stars, date and/or "LIBERTY."

GOOD

The rim may be worn down to the tops of the stars and legend. Head will be well outlined but worn flat.

VERY FINE
Wear will be apparent on the top half of the bottom leaves.

EXTREMELY FINE
There will be wear on the ends of the leaves and ribbon bow.

Note: There may be weakness at the top of the wreath due to striking. This weakness should not alter the condition of the coin.

ABOUT UNCIRCULATED
Only a trace of wear will be visible on the ribbon bow and the tips of the leaves.

DRAPED BUST DIMES 1796-1807

(For 1796-1797 reverses see page 81)

ABOUT GOOD
The rim will be worn down well into the legend and design.

GOOD
The rim will be worn down into the tops of some of the letters. The eagle will be clear but show no detail.

95

VERY GOOD

About one-third of the hair detail will show. Some evidence of drapery lines will be visible.

Note: Some spots may show more wear than surrounding areas due to uneven striking and should not alter the condition of the coin.

FINE

Approximately half of the hair detail will show.

VERY FINE

About three-quarters of the hair detail will show.

EXTREMELY FINE

Almost all of the hair detail will be visible but may not be sharp due to striking.

ABOUT UNCIRCULATED

Only a trace of wear will be visible on Liberty's shoulder and highest points of hair.

VERY GOOD

A few feathers will show in the eagle's wings.
A partial "E PLURIBUS UNUM" will show.

FINE

Approximately half of the feathers will show.
"E PLURIBUS UNUM" will be complete but
may have a weak letter or two.

VERY FINE

About three-quarters of the feathers will show
and be sharp.

EXTREMELY FINE

Wear will appear on the breast, tail and at the
ends of the wings.

ABOUT UNCIRCULATED

Only a trace of wear will appear on the breast,
tail and at the tips of the wings.

Note: There may be weakness near the rim
of both the obverse and reverse due to striking
(especially in 1807). This should not affect the
overall grade of the coin.

ABOUT GOOD
The rim will be worn down well into the stars and/or date. The head will be worn smooth.

GOOD
The rim may be worn down to the tops of the stars (usually on only one side). The head will be well outlined.

VERY GOOD
A total of any three letters of "LIBERTY" will be visible. The rim will be full.

FINE
A full "LIBERTY" will show. The ear will be visible.

VERY FINE
"LIBERTY" will be very sharp. About two-thirds of the hair will show.

CAPPED DIMES 1809-1837

ABOUT GOOD
The rim will be worn down well into the letters.

GOOD
All of the letters will be readable although a few of them may be weak.

VERY GOOD
All of the letters will be sharp. A partial "E PLURIBUS UNUM" will show.

FINE
There will be a full "E PLURIBUS UNUM." About half of the eagle's feathers will show.

VERY FINE
"E PLURIBUS UNUM" will be sharp. Almost all of the feathers will show but wear will be visible on the high points.

EXTREMELY FINE

All of the hair will show but be worn on the highest points of the curls and around the face.

ABOUT UNCIRCULATED

Only a trace of wear will show on the shoulder and the hair above the ear and forehead.

Note: The clasp of Liberty's wrap may be weak due to striking and therefore cannot be used to determine condition.

DIMES 1837-1838 (no stars)

ABOUT GOOD

The rim will be worn down into the field and may be worn into the date and/or head.

GOOD

There will be a full outline of Liberty. The shield will be worn smooth.

VERY GOOD

A total of any three letters of "LIBERTY" will be visible on the shield.

EXTREMELY FINE

Wear will be visible on the highest points of the feathers, claws and neck.

ABOUT UNCIRCULATED

Only a trace of wear will be visible on the eagle's neck, left claw and the tips of the wings.

DIMES 1837-1838 (no stars)

ABOUT GOOD

Approximately half of the lettering will be visible.

GOOD

The rim will be worn down to the tops of some of the letters.

VERY GOOD

There will be a full rim. The leaves in the wreath will be outlined but not well defined.

FINE

There will be a full "LIBERTY" on the shield but it will not be sharp.

VERY FINE

"LIBERTY" will be sharp. Only the deepest folds of Liberty's gown will be visible.

EXTREMELY FINE

There will be wear on Liberty's breast and legs.

ABOUT UNCIRCULATED

Only a trace of wear will appear on Liberty's breast and knees.

Note: The horizontal lines of the shield are often weak even on higher grades due to striking.

LIBERTY SEATED DIMES 1838-1860

ABOUT GOOD

The rim will be worn down into the date and/or stars.

FINE
The leaves will be separated but will show little detail.

VERY FINE
Approximately half of the leaves will show detail.

EXTREMELY FINE
All of the leaves show detail but will have wear on the ends.

ABOUT UNCIRCULATED
Only a trace of wear will be visible on the ribbon bow and the tips of the leaves.

LIBERTY SEATED DIMES 1838-1860

ABOUT GOOD
About half of the lettering will be visible.

GOOD

There will be a full outline of Liberty. The shield will be worn smooth.

VERY GOOD

A total of any three letters of "LIBERTY" will be visible on the shield.

FINE

There will be a full "LIBERTY" on the shield but it will not be sharp.

VERY FINE

"LIBERTY" will be sharp. Only the deepest folds of Liberty's gown will be visible.

EXTREMELY FINE

There will be wear on Liberty's head, breast and legs.

GOOD
All of the lettering will be full and sharp. The wreath will be worn flat.

VERY GOOD
The leaves in the wreath will be outlined but not well defined.

FINE
The leaves will be separated but not show much detail.

VERY FINE
Approximately half of the leaves will show detail.

EXTREMELY FINE
All of the leaves show detail but will have wear on the ends.

ABOUT UNCIRCULATED

Only a trace of wear will appear on Liberty's breast and knees.

Note: The clasp of Liberty's gown may be weak due to striking and therefore cannot be used to determine condition.

LIBERTY SEATED DIMES 1860-1891

ABOUT GOOD

The rim will be worn down into the letters and/or date.

GOOD

There will be a full rim. "LIBERTY" will not show.

VERY GOOD

A total of any three letters of "LIBERTY" will be visible.

FINE

There will be a full "LIBERTY" but it will not be sharp. The deepest folds of Liberty's gown will be visible.

ABOUT UNCIRCULATED

Only a trace of wear will be visible on the ribbon bow and the tips of the leaves.

LIBERTY SEATED DIMES 1860-1891

ABOUT GOOD

The rim will be worn down into the wreath.

GOOD

The wreath will be well outlined but worn flat.

VERY GOOD

Individual leaves will be outlined but show very little detail.

FINE

All of the major detail will be visible but show definite wear.

VERY FINE

"LIBERTY" will be sharp. More detail will be visible on the upper folds of Liberty's gown.

EXTREMELY FINE

There will be wear on Liberty's head, breast and legs.

ABOUT UNCIRCULATED

Only a trace of wear will appear on Liberty's breast and knees.

BARBER DIMES 1892-1916

ABOUT GOOD

The rim will be worn down into the letters and/or date.

GOOD

The letters will be complete. The head will be well outlined but worn smooth.

VERY FINE

Sharper detail will appear on the leaves of the wreath.

EXTREMELY FINE

There will be wear only on the high points of the wreath.

ABOUT UNCIRCULATED

Only a trace of wear will be visible on the tips of the leaves.

Note: There may be weakness at the top of the wreath due to striking. This weakness should not alter the condition of the coin.

BARBER DIMES 1892-1916

ABOUT GOOD

The rim will be worn down into the wreath.

GOOD

The wreath will be outlined but worn flat.

109

VERY GOOD

A total of any three letters of "LIBERTY" will show.

FINE

There will be a full "LIBERTY" on the head but it will not be sharp. The top of the wreath will be well outlined but the bottom will be worn.

VERY FINE

"LIBERTY" will be sharp. The wreath will be well outlined at both top and bottom.

EXTREMELY FINE

The edges of the band on which "LIBERTY" appears will be distinct. The wreath will be bold. There will be wear above the forehead.

ABOUT UNCIRCULATED

Only a trace of wear will appear on the hair above the forehead, the tips of the leaves in the wreath and on the cheek bone.

VERY GOOD

Individual leaves will be outlined but show very little detail.

FINE

All of the major detail will be visible but show definite wear.

VERY FINE

Sharper detail will appear on the leaves of the wreath.

EXTREMELY FINE

There will be wear only on the high points of the wreath.

ABOUT UNCIRCULATED

Only a trace of wear will be visible on the tips of the leaves.

111

MERCURY DIMES 1916-1945

ABOUT GOOD

The rim will be worn down halfway into the letters and date. Head will be worn smooth.

GOOD

The rim will touch the tops of the letters and the bottom of the last digit in the date. The wing will be flat.

VERY GOOD

All of the letters and the date will be clear of the rim. There will be a few feathers on the wing.

FINE

The rim will be sharp. About half of the feathers of the wing will be visible. Hair braid around face will be worn smooth at the bottom.

VERY FINE

Approximately three-quarters of the feathers will be visible. The hair braid will show more detail.

112

MERCURY DIMES 1916-1945

ABOUT GOOD

The rim will be worn halfway into the letters and will touch the bottom of the mint mark (if any).

GOOD

The rim will be worn down to the tops of the letters. The fasces will be worn smooth.

VERY GOOD

The rim will be full. Half of the vertical lines in the fasces will show.

FINE

All of the vertical lines will show but not sharply. The two diagonal bands will show across the fasces but will be worn smooth in the middle.

VERY FINE

All of the vertical lines will be sharp. The two diagonal bands will be complete across the fasces.

EXTREMELY FINE

All of the feathers will show but be worn on the high points. Hair braid will be well detailed.

ABOUT UNCIRCULATED

Only a trace of wear will be visible on the hair braid and at the connection of the wing to the head.

ROOSEVELT DIMES 1946 to date

GOOD

There will be a full rim. Hair will be worn smooth. The ear will be worn flat.

VERY GOOD

Approximately one-fourth of the hair will show.

FINE

Half of the hair will show. The ear will be sharp.

EXTREMELY FINE

The two diagonal bands will be raised across the fasces. The center horizontal bands will be sharp but not separated.

ABOUT UNCIRCULATED

Only a trace of wear will appear in the center of the diagonal bands. The center horizontal bands will be separated but show a trace of wear.

ROOSEVELT DIMES 1946 to date

GOOD

The rim will be worn down to the tops of the letters. The torch will be worn smooth.

VERY GOOD

Only the lines at the side of the torch will show.

FINE

Half of the lines in the torch will show.

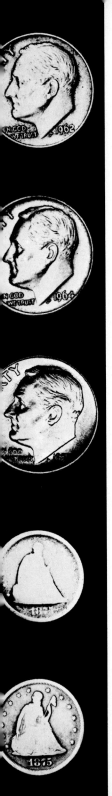

VERY FINE

Most of the major detail of the hair will be visible but worn on the high points and around the face.

EXTREMELY FINE

All of the hair detail will show but will have slight wear to the right of the forehead and above the ear. The ear will show complete detail.

ABOUT UNCIRCULATED

Only a trace of wear will show on the cheekbone and on the hair above the ear.

TWENTY CENT PIECES 1875-1878

ABOUT GOOD

The rim will be worn down into the stars.

GOOD

There will be a full rim. The shield will be worn smooth.

116

VERY FINE
Two-thirds of the lines in the torch will show.

EXTREMELY FINE
All of the lines in the torch will show. The flame will be well detailed.

ABOUT UNCIRCULATED
Only a trace of wear will show on the tops of the leaves and the high point of the flame.

TWENTY CENT PIECES 1875-1878

ABOUT GOOD
The rim will be worn well down into the letters.

GOOD
There will be a full rim. The eagle will be worn almost smooth.

VERY GOOD

One or two letters of "LIBERTY" will show.

Note: On the twenty cent piece the word "LIBERTY" is raised instead of incused as on the Liberty seated dime, quarter or half dollar. Therefore, different grading standards must be used for this coin.

FINE

Most of the word "LIBERTY" will show but be very weak in spots. The major details of Liberty's gown will show.

VERY FINE

There will be a full "LIBERTY." Liberty's gown will show considerable detail.

EXTREMELY FINE

"LIBERTY" will be very sharp. There will be wear on the breast and legs.

ABOUT UNCIRCULATED

Only a trace of wear will appear on the head, breast and knees.

VERY GOOD

Approximately half of the feathers will show on the eagle. The center of the breast will be worn smooth.

FINE

Almost all of the feathers will show. There will be a smooth spot in the center of the eagle's breast.

VERY FINE

All of the feathers will be visible but will show wear on the high points.

EXTREMELY FINE

There will be wear on the eagle's breast, left leg and tops of the wings.

ABOUT UNCIRCULATED

Only a trace of wear will appear on the eagle's breast and tops of the wings.

Note: The top of the eagle's right wing often appears flat even on uncirculated coins due to striking.

ABOUT GOOD

The rim will be worn down well into the stars and "LIBERTY."

GOOD

The rim may be worn down to the tops of a few letters and/or stars. The head will be worn smooth.

VERY GOOD

The head will be well outlined with the top and bottom curls distinct. No hair detail will show around the face or neck.

FINE

About half of the major hair detail will show. There will be hair detail around the ear and to the left of the neck.

VERY FINE

Approximately two-thirds of the hair detail will show.

DRAPED BUST QUARTERS 1796-1807

(For 1796 reverse see page 171)

ABOUT GOOD

The rim will be worn down well into the lettering and design.

GOOD

The rim will be worn down into the tops of some of the letters. The eagle's wings will be worn smooth.

VERY GOOD

A few feathers will show in the wings. A partial "E PLURIBUS UNUM" will show.

FINE

Approximately half of the eagle's feathers will show.

VERY FINE

Three-fourths of the eagle's feathers will be visible. "E PLURIBUS UNUM" will be sharp.

121

EXTREMELY FINE
All of the major hair detail will show.

ABOUT UNCIRCULATED
Only a trace of wear will show on the shoulder and the highest waves of hair to the left of the ear and forehead.

Note: The obverse of this series appears to be struck more softly than other denominations of this period.

LARGE CAPPED QUARTERS 1815-1828

ABOUT GOOD
The rim will be worn down well into the stars.

Note: There may be a partial "LIBERTY" even in very low grades.

GOOD
The rim will be worn down to the tops of the stars.

VERY GOOD
There will be a full rim. At least 3 full letters of "LIBERTY" must show.

EXTREMELY FINE

All of the major details of the feathers will show but be weak at the ends.

Note: The eagle's wing just to the right of the shield may be weak due to striking.

ABOUT UNCIRCULATED

Only a trace of wear will appear on the eagle's breast feathers and at the tips of the wings.

Note: The shield detail may be uneven due to striking.

LARGE CAPPED QUARTERS 1815-1828

ABOUT GOOD

The rim will be worn down well into the letters.

GOOD

The rim may be worn down to the tops of some letters. The eagle's feathers and the banner on which "E PLURIBUS UNUM" appears will be worn smooth.

VERY GOOD

A partial "E PLURIBUS UNUM" will show.

FINE

"LIBERTY" will be complete and sharp. Half of the major hair detail will show. All of the curls will be worn on the high points.

VERY FINE

The hair will be more detailed. Drapery will be well outlined.

EXTREMELY FINE

All of the hair will be detailed but show wear on the high points.

ABOUT UNCIRCULATED

Only a trace of wear will show on the hair above the eye and ear and the tips of the curls.

Note: This series may be weakly struck around the curl on the neck and the drapery clasp therefore the overall grade of the coin cannot be determined by these features.

SMALL CAPPED QUARTERS 1831-1838

ABOUT GOOD

The rim will be worn down into the stars and/or date. The head will be worn smooth.

FINE
There will be a full "E PLURIBUS UNUM" although a few letters may be weakly struck.

VERY FINE
"E PLURIBUS UNUM" will be sharp. About two-thirds of the eagle's feathers will show.

EXTREMELY FINE
All of the feathers will be visible but the edges of the wings will show wear.

ABOUT UNCIRCULATED
There will be a slight trace of wear on the tips of the wings and the claws.

SMALL CAPPED QUARTERS 1831-1838

ABOUT GOOD
The rim will be worn down into the letters. The eagle's feathers will be worn smooth.

GOOD

The stars and date will be full. There may be a partial "LIBERTY."

VERY GOOD

There will be a full "LIBERTY" but a letter or two may be weak. Half of the major detail of the hair will show.

FINE

"LIBERTY" will be strong. All of the major hair detail will show but the curls will be worn flat.

VERY FINE

The hair curls will show less wear and appear more rounded.

EXTREMELY FINE

Wear will appear on the highest hair curls and the top of Liberty's cap.

ABOUT UNCIRCULATED

Only a trace of wear will show at the top and bottom tips of the wings and the eagle's left claw.

LIBERTY SEATED QUARTERS 1838-1891

ABOUT GOOD

The rim will be worn down well into the lettering.

GOOD

All lettering will be clear. The eagle will be worn smooth.

VERY GOOD

The rim will be sharply defined. A few feathers will show on the eagle.

FINE

About half of the eagle's feathers will show.

VERY FINE

"LIBERTY" will be sharp. Only the deepest folds of Liberty's gown will be visible.

EXTREMELY FINE

More detail of Liberty's gown will show. There will be wear on Liberty's head, breast and legs.

ABOUT UNCIRCULATED

Only a trace of wear will appear on Liberty's breast and knees.

Note: The clasp of Liberty's gown may be weak due to striking and therefore cannot be used to determine condition.

BARBER QUARTERS 1892-1916

ABOUT GOOD

The rim will be worn down into the stars, letters and/or date.

GOOD

The stars, letters and date will be complete. The head will be well outlined but worn smooth.

VERY FINE

Three-quarters of the feathers will be visible. Wear will show on the neck, leg and edges of the wings.

EXTREMELY FINE

All of the major details will be visible but be worn on the high points. The neck and claws will show slight wear.

ABOUT UNCIRCULATED

Only a trace of wear will show on the neck, the claws and the tops of the wings.

Note: Flat spots will sometimes occur due to striking.

BARBER QUARTERS 1892-1916

ABOUT GOOD

The rim will be worn down into the lettering.

GOOD

The rim may be worn down to the tops of a few letters. The eagle will be well outlined but worn smooth.

VERY GOOD

A total of any three letters of "LIBERTY" will show.

FINE

There will be a full "LIBERTY" on the head but it will not be sharp. The top of the wreath will be well outlined but the bottom will be worn.

VERY FINE

"LIBERTY" will be sharp. The wreath will be well outlined at both top and bottom.

EXTREMELY FINE

The edges of the band on which "LIBERTY" appears will be distinct. The wreath will be bold. There will be wear above the forehead.

ABOUT UNCIRCULATED

Only a trace of wear will appear on the hair above the forehead, the tips of the leaves in the wreath and on the cheekbone.

VERY GOOD

A few feathers will show in the wings. A partial "E PLURIBUS UNUM" will show.

FINE

Approximately half of the feathers will show. "E PLURIBUS UNUM" will be three-quarters complete.

VERY FINE

"E PLURIBUS UNUM" will be complete. More feather detail will show on the neck and tail.

EXTREMELY FINE

All of the major detail of the feathers will show. Wear will be apparent on the neck, tail and upper edges of the wings.

ABOUT UNCIRCULATED

Only a trace of wear will be visible on the eagle's head, tail and tips of the wings.

LIBERTY STANDING QUARTERS 1916-1917

ABOUT GOOD
The date will be identifiable although it will be barely visible.

GOOD
The top portion of the date will be worn smooth. Date will easily be identified.

VERY GOOD
The date will be complete but the very top will be weak. The band of cloth from Liberty's right hand to the shield will be outlined.

FINE
The date will be sharp. The shield will be complete around its outer edge. Liberty's right leg will be worn flat.

VERY FINE
Liberty's right leg will be rounded but worn from above the gown to midway between the foot and knee. The gown line in the center of the upper leg will be worn.

ABOUT GOOD

The rim will be worn down into the lettering and stars.

GOOD

All of the lettering will be clear. The eagle will be outlined sharply but worn almost smooth.

VERY GOOD

One-third of the feathers will show.

FINE

Half of the feathers will show.

VERY FINE

Almost all the major detail of the feathers will show. The eagle's body and the front edge of the right wing will be worn flat.

EXTREMELY FINE

Liberty's right leg will be worn on the knee. The gown line will be visible across the leg. The breast will be rounded.

ABOUT UNCIRCULATED

Only a trace of wear will show on the knee cap, head and center of shield.

LIBERTY STANDING QUARTERS 1917-1924

ABOUT GOOD

The date will be identifiable although it will be barely visible.

GOOD

Wear will extend into the date but the date will be easily identified.

Note: The date was on a higher plane from 1917-1924 therefore grading of this series from About Good to Fine should be determined by the wear on the date.

VERY GOOD

The date will be complete but may be weak. The band of cloth from Liberty's right hand to the shield will be outlined on top.

136

EXTREMELY FINE

There will be wear on only the highest point of the front edge of the right wing. Wear will be visible on the highest points of the eagle's body.

ABOUT UNCIRCULATED

Only a trace of wear will be seen on the highest point of the eagle's body.

LIBERTY STANDING QUARTERS 1917-1924

ABOUT GOOD

The rim may be worn down to the tops of some letters.

Note: Since the lower conditions of this series are basically determined by the date the reverses appear to be in better condition than on quarters of 1925-1930.

GOOD

The rim will be worn down to the tops of the letters.

VERY GOOD

There will be a full rim. About one-third of the feathers will show.

137

FINE

The date will be sharp. The shield will be complete around its outer edge. Liberty's right leg will be worn flat.

VERY FINE

Liberty's right leg will be rounded but worn from above the gown to the foot. About half of the mail covering the breast will show.

EXTREMELY FINE

Liberty's right knee and the tip of her breast will show slight wear.

ABOUT UNCIRCULATED

Only a trace of wear will show on the knee cap, breast and center of shield.

Note: This series was usually struck with a flat head. An Uncirculated coin with a fully detailed head is worth a premium price.

LIBERTY STANDING QUARTERS 1925-1930

ABOUT GOOD

The rim will be worn down into the date and letters.

FINE
Approximately half of the feathers will show.

VERY FINE
The eagle's body will be worn smooth.

EXTREMELY FINE
All of the feathers will show but will be worn on the high spots.

ABOUT UNCIRCULATED
Only a trace of wear will show on the front edge of the eagle's wing and the high points of the breast.

LIBERTY STANDING QUARTERS 1925-1930

ABOUT GOOD
The rim will be worn down into the lettering and stars.

GOOD
There will be a full date. Liberty will be worn smooth.

VERY GOOD
More detail will appear in the folds of Liberty's gown and her shield.

FINE
The shield will be complete around its outer edge. Liberty's right leg will be worn flat.

VERY FINE
About half of the mail covering the breast will show.

EXTREMELY FINE
Liberty's right knee and the tip of her breast will show slight wear.

GOOD

The rim will be worn down to the tops of the letters.

VERY GOOD

There will be a full rim. About one-third of the feathers will show.

FINE

Approximately half of the feathers will show.

VERY FINE

The eagle's body will be worn smooth.

EXTREMELY FINE

All of the feathers will show but will be worn on the high spots.

ABOUT UNCIRCULATED

Only a trace of wear will show on Liberty's right knee and breast.

Note: Usually struck with a flat head.

WASHINGTON QUARTERS 1932 to date

ABOUT GOOD

The rim will be worn halfway into the letters and date.

GOOD

The rim will be worn into the tops of the letters and the bottom of the date.

VERY GOOD

The rim will touch the tops of the letters and the bottom of the date.

FINE

There will be a full rim. The hairline will begin to show above the forehead.

ABOUT UNCIRCULATED

Only a trace of wear will show on the front edge of the eagle's wing and the high points of the breast.

WASHINGTON QUARTERS 1932 to date

ABOUT GOOD

The rim will be worn halfway down into the letters.

GOOD

The rim will be worn down into the tops of the letters.

VERY GOOD

The rim will touch the tops of some of the letters.

FINE

There will be a full rim. No feathers will show on the eagle's breast.

VERY FINE

The major details of the hair will show but there will be considerable wear on the curls.

Note: The motto "IN GOD WE TRUST" is weakly struck on all 1932 and some 1934 issues.

EXTREMELY FINE

The hair on the highest points of the head and curls will show wear.

ABOUT UNCIRCULATED

Only a trace of wear on the cheek, the high points of the hair and around the ear.

FLOWING HAIR HALF DOLLARS 1794-1795

ABOUT GOOD

The rim will be worn down well into the design.

GOOD

The head will be well outlined but show almost no detail. There may be a few weak spots around the rim.

144

VERY FINE

Feathers will show on both sides of the eagle's breast.

EXTREMELY FINE

There will be wear on the high points of the eagle's breast and legs.

ABOUT UNCIRCULATED

Only a trace of wear will be visible on the eagle's breast and tops of the legs.

FLOWING HAIR HALF DOLLARS 1794-1795

ABOUT GOOD

The rim will be worn down well into the letters and design.

GOOD

The rim may be worn down into the tops of some of the letters. The eagle will be outlined but worn completely smooth.

145

VERY GOOD

All of the lettering and date will be clear. About one-quarter of the hair detail will show.

FINE

About half of the detail will show in the hair. The top of the head will be worn smooth.

VERY FINE

Approximately two-thirds of the hair will show and be outlined around the forehead.

EXTREMELY FINE

Almost all of the hair will show. The top of the head will still show a few wear spots.

Note: This series was generally softly struck so the fine detail may not show even on high grade specimens.

ABOUT UNCIRCULATED

All of the hair will show. Only a slight trace of wear will show on the bust and highest waves of hair.

146

VERY GOOD
The breast of the eagle is outlined against the wings.

FINE
Some feathers will show on the eagle's left wing and tail.

VERY FINE
About half of the feathers will show. The leaves will be well defined.

EXTREMELY FINE
Three-quarters of the feathers will show. The leaves will be well rounded but worn on the high points.

ABOUT UNCIRCULATED
A trace of wear will show on the top edges of the wings, breast and head. The leaves will be well detailed.

Note: The breast feathers were usually weakly struck on this series.

DRAPED BUST HALF DOLLARS 1796-1807

ABOUT GOOD

The rim will be worn down into the letters, stars and date.

GOOD

The letters, stars and date will be clear. The head will be outlined but worn smooth.

VERY GOOD

About one-third of the hairlines will show.

FINE

More detail will show in the hair which will be two-thirds complete.

VERY FINE

About three-quarters of the hairlines will be visible.

148

DRAPED BUST HALF DOLLARS 1796-1807

(For 1796-1797 reverses see page 171)

ABOUT GOOD

The rim will be worn down into the lettering and design.

GOOD

The lettering will be clear although the rim may be worn down to the tops of a few letters. The wings will be worn smooth.

VERY GOOD

A partial "E PLURIBUS UNUM" will show. A few feathers will be visible.

FINE

"E PLURIBUS UNUM" will be complete but a few letters may be weak.

VERY FINE

"E PLURIBUS UNUM" will be strong. About three-quarters of the feathers will show.

EXTREMELY FINE

All of the major hair details will show. There will be flatness due to wear above the forehead and on the back of the head.

ABOUT UNCIRCULATED

Only a trace of wear will show on the highest points of hair, cheek and shoulder.

CAPPED HALF DOLLARS 1807-1836

ABOUT GOOD

The rim will be worn down into the stars and date.

GOOD

The head will be outlined but show no detail. There will be a partial "LIBERTY."

VERY GOOD

A full "LIBERTY" will show. About half of the major hair detail will be visible.

150

EXTREMELY FINE

All of the major details of the feathers will show. The ends and top edges of the wings will show wear.

ABOUT UNCIRCULATED

Only a trace of wear will show on the top edges and tips of the wings, breast, head and tail.

CAPPED HALF DOLLARS 1807-1836

ABOUT GOOD

The rim will be worn down into the letters.

GOOD

All of the letters will be complete. The eagle will be outlined but worn smooth.

VERY GOOD

A few feathers will be visible in the eagle's left wing.

FINE
About two-thirds of the major hair detail will show.

VERY FINE
All of the major hair detail will show. The tops of the waves of hair will be worn flat.

EXTREMELY FINE
The hair curls will be well rounded with wear only on the high points.

Note: The drapery clasp often comes quite weak due to striking even on higher grade specimens and should not be used to determine grade.

ABOUT UNCIRCULATED
Only a trace of wear will appear on the cheek, cap and highest waves of hair above the forehead and ear.

REEDED EDGE HALF DOLLARS 1836-1839

ABOUT GOOD
The rim will be worn down well into the stars and date.

FINE

Half of the feathers will show. The eagle's claws will be well outlined but show wear.

VERY FINE

Nearly all the major details of the feathers will show. Definite wear will show on the high points of the feathers.

EXTREMELY FINE

All of the feathers will be clearly visible. There will be slight wear on the highest tips of the feathers, tops of the wings and the claws.

ABOUT UNCIRCULATED

Only a trace of wear will show on the claws, the tops of the wings and the head.

Note: Weakness resulting from a weak strike will sometimes obliterate part of "E PLURIBUS UNUM" and the upper right wing. This weakness should not alter the grade.

REEDED EDGE HALF DOLLARS 1836-1839

ABOUT GOOD

The rim will be worn down well into the letters.

GOOD

The head will be outlined but worn almost completely smooth. There will be a partial "LIBERTY" showing.

VERY GOOD

There will be a full "LIBERTY." A few waves of hair will show.

FINE

About half of the major hair details will show.

VERY FINE

All of the major hair detail will show but the tops of the waves of hair will be worn flat.

EXTREMELY FINE

The hair curls will be well rounded with wear only on the high points.

GOOD

The eagle will be outlined but show no feathers.

Note: The lettering on the 1836 and 1837 halves will be quite weak due to a low rim. This must be taken into consideration when grading these dates.

VERY GOOD

A few feathers will be visible.

FINE

Approximately half of the feathers will show.

VERY FINE

Three-quarters of the feathers will show.

EXTREMELY FINE

All of the feathers will be clearly visible but wear will show on the high points. The claws and the edges of the wings will show wear.

ABOUT UNCIRCULATED

Only a trace of wear will appear on the cheek, ear, cap and hair above the forehead.

LIBERTY SEATED HALF DOLLARS 1839-1891

ABOUT GOOD

The rim will be worn down into the date and/or stars.

GOOD

There will be a full outline of Liberty. The shield will be worn smooth.

VERY GOOD

A total of any three letters of "LIBERTY" will be visible on the shield.

FINE

There will be a full "LIBERTY" on the shield but it will not be sharp.

ABOUT UNCIRCULATED

Only a trace of wear will be visible on the highest part of the edges of the wings, the head and the claws.

LIBERTY SEATED HALF DOLLARS 1839-1891

ABOUT GOOD

The rim will be worn down well into the letters.

GOOD

The letters will be complete although the rim may be worn down to the tops of a few letters. The eagle will be worn smooth.

VERY GOOD

The rim will be complete. A few feathers will show in the wings.

FINE

About half of the eagle's feathers will show.

VERY FINE

"LIBERTY" will be sharp. Only the deepest folds of Liberty's gown will be visible.

EXTREMELY FINE

More detail of Liberty's gown will show. There will be wear on Liberty's head, breast and legs.

ABOUT UNCIRCULATED

Only a trace of wear will appear on Liberty's breast and knees.

Note: The clasp of Liberty's gown may be weak due to striking and therefore cannot be used to determine condition.

BARBER HALF DOLLARS 1892-1915

ABOUT GOOD

The rim will be worn down into the stars, letters and/or date.

GOOD

The stars, letters and date will be complete. The head will be well outlined but worn smooth.

ABOUT GOOD
Rim worn down into letters.

GOOD
Rim worn down to tops of letters.

VERY GOOD
Full rim. A few feathers will show.

FINE
Half the feathers will show.

VERY FINE
All wing feathers will show. Breast worn smooth.

EXTREMELY FINE

There will be light wear on the head, breast and left leg.

ABOUT UNCIRCULATED

Only a trace of wear will show on the highest points of the head, breast and left arm.

FRANKLIN HALF DOLLARS 1948-1963

GOOD

The rim will be worn down into the lettering.

VERY GOOD

There will be a full rim. Hair behind the ear will be worn smooth.

FINE

Some hair detail will show behind the ear. The cheek will be worn flat.

EXTREMELY FINE
High point of breast and left leg worn.

ABOUT UNCIRCULATED
Trace of wear on breast, leg and wing tip.

FRANKLIN HALF DOLLARS 1948-1963

GOOD
The rim will be worn down into the lettering.

VERY GOOD
The rim will be worn down to the tops of the letters.

FINE
There will be a full rim.

VERY FINE

All of the major hairlines will show. The cheek will show wear but will be well rounded.

EXTREMELY FINE

More hair detail will show.

ABOUT UNCIRCULATED

Only a trace of wear will be visible on the cheek, shoulder and hair to the left of the ear.

KENNEDY HALF DOLLARS 1964 to date

EXTREMELY FINE

Wear will appear on the cheek and highest portion of hair to the right of the forehead.

Note: Kennedy half dollars are rarely seen in less than Extremely Fine condition.

ABOUT UNCIRCULATED

Only a trace of wear will show on the cheek and highest portion of the hair.

VERY FINE

About half of the horizontal lines on the bell will show.

EXTREMELY FINE

Two-thirds of the horizontal lines will show.

ABOUT UNCIRCULATED

Only a trace of wear will show on the top of the bell and on the horizontal lines.

KENNEDY HALF DOLLARS 1964 to date

EXTREMELY FINE

The head, shield, tail and the top edges of the wings will show.

Note: Kennedy half dollars are rarely seen in less than Extremely Fine condition.

ABOUT UNCIRCULATED

Just a trace of wear will appear on the neck and highest point of the tail.

FLOWING HAIR DOLLARS 1794-1795

ABOUT GOOD
The rim will be worn down into the stars, legend and/or date.

GOOD
Liberty's head will be outlined but show no details. The stars, legend and date will be clearly readable.

VERY GOOD
Major facial details will be visible. The bottom strands of hair will show.

FINE
Approximately half of the major hair detail will show.

VERY FINE
Two-thirds of the hair detail will show.

FLOWING HAIR DOLLARS 1794-1795

ABOUT GOOD
The rim will be worn down into the lettering.

GOOD
The rim will be worn down to the tops of some of the lettering. The eagle will be worn smooth.

VERY GOOD
The eagle's outline and the feathers around the body will be visible. The wings will be worn smooth.

FINE
The major feather details will show in the eagle's right wing.

VERY FINE
Approximately half of the feather detail will show.

EXTREMELY FINE

All of the major hair detail will be visible. The hair around the face and forehead will show wear.

ABOUT UNCIRCULATED

Only a trace of wear will show on the tips of the highest curls and on the hair to the left of the forehead.

DRAPED BUST DOLLARS 1795-1804

ABOUT GOOD

The rim will be worn down into the stars, legend and/or date.

GOOD

The head will be boldly outlined. There will be a full rim.

VERY GOOD

The bottom and top curls will show some detail. The rest of the hair will be worn smooth.

170

EXTREMELY FINE

All of the major feather detail will be visible on the wings and tail. The breast will be smooth. The tips and edges of the wings will show wear.

ABOUT UNCIRCULATED

Only a trace of wear will show on the head, breast and tops of the wings.

Note: The breast feathers were usually weakly struck on this series.

DRAPED BUST DOLLARS
1795-1804

ABOUT GOOD
Rim will be worn down into the letters.

GOOD
All letters will be readable.

VERY GOOD
Full rim. Partial "E PLU-RIBUS UNUM" (on large eagle).

171

FINE

Approximately half of the hair detail will show.

Note: Drapery line details vary too much from one variety to another to be accurately used to determine grade.

VERY FINE

Two-thirds of the hair detail will show.

EXTREMELY FINE

All of the major hair detail will show. The highest waves of hair to the left of the neck and forehead will be worn.

ABOUT UNCIRCULATED

Only a trace of wear will show on the bust, shoulder and the hair left of the forehead.

LIBERTY SEATED DOLLARS 1840-1873

ABOUT GOOD

The rim will be worn down into the date and/or stars.

FINE

Half of the feathers will show. "E PLURIBUS UNUM" (on large eagle) will be full but weak.

VERY FINE

Three-quarters of the feathers will show.

EXTREMELY FINE

Slight wear on breast and top edges of wings.

ABOUT UNCIRCULATED

Traces of wear on breast and extreme top edges of wings.

DOLLARS 1840-1873

UT GOOD

, down well into the letters.

GOOD

There will be a full rim. Liberty will be sharply outlined. The shield will be worn smooth.

VERY GOOD

A total of any three letters of "LIBERTY" will show on the shield. A few major gown lines will show.

FINE

The "LI" and "TY" of "LIBERTY" will be clearly visible but only the top of "BER" will show.

Note: The shield is raised higher on this series and thus shows wear more quickly than on the Liberty Seated dime, quarter or half. Therefore, different grading standards must be used for this coin.

VERY FINE

"LIBERTY" will be complete with weakness showing only at the bottom part of "BE." All of the major gown lines will show.

EXTREMELY FINE

"LIBERTY" will be sharp. The breast will be outlined but worn on the high points. The head and Liberty's right leg will show wear.

GOOD
The letters will be complete although the rim may be worn down to the tops of a few letters. The eagle will be worn smooth.

VERY GOOD
The rim will be complete. A few feathers will show on the wings.

FINE
About half of the eagle's feathers will show.

VERY FINE
Nearly all of the major details of the feathers will show. Definite wear will show on the high points of the feathers.

EXTREMELY FINE
All of the feathers will be plainly visible. There will be slight wear on the highest tips of the feathers, the tops of the wings and the claws.

ABOUT UNCIRCULATED

Only a trace of wear will show on the head, knee and tips of the breasts.

MORGAN DOLLARS 1878-1921

GOOD

The hair above the forehead and ear will be worn smooth.

VERY GOOD

The deepest strands of hair will be visible above the forehead. The hair above the ear will be worn smooth.

FINE

Approximately half of the hairlines will show from the top of the head to the ear.

VERY FINE

Three-quarters of the hairlines will show. The high points of the bottom curls will show considerable wear.

ABOUT UNCIRCULATED

Only a trace of wear will show on the claws, head and the tops of the wings.

MORGAN DOLLARS 1878-1921

GOOD

The rim will be worn down to the tops of the letters.

VERY GOOD

Approximately one-third of the feathers will show on the eagle. The head and breast will be worn smooth.

FINE

Three-quarters of the major feather detail will show on the wings. The breast will be worn smooth.

VERY FINE

All of the feathers will show on the wings. There will be wear on the center breast feathers and the top edges of the wings.

177

EXTREMELY FINE

All of the hairlines will show. Wear will appear on the high points around the ear.

ABOUT UNCIRCULATED

Only a trace of wear will show on the hair just above the ear and the high points of hair above the forehead.

PEACE DOLLARS 1921-1935

VERY GOOD

The head will be worn smooth.

Note: This coin rarely comes in grades less than Very Good.

FINE

The high waves of hair above the forehead and ear will be worn flat.

VERY FINE

The hair above the forehead will be worn.

Note: The word "GOD" was often weakly struck. This does not alter the grade.

178

EXTREMELY FINE
There will be wear on the head and the highest points of the breast feathers.

ABOUT UNCIRCULATED
Only a trace of wear will show on the highest points of the breast and head.

PEACE DOLLARS 1921-1935

VERY GOOD
The word "PEACE" will show although a few letters may be weak.

FINE
The right wing will be outlined but only a few feathers will show.

VERY FINE
The major feather details will show. Considerable wear will cause flatness on the right wing and head.

EXTREMELY FINE
All of the hairlines will show. There will be some flatness on the highest waves of hair from wear.

ABOUT UNCIRCULATED
Only a trace of wear will show on Liberty's cheek and the highest waves of her hair above the forehead and ear.

TRADE DOLLARS 1873-1885

GOOD
Liberty will be well outlined but worn almost smooth.

VERY GOOD
A partial "IN GOD WE TRUST" will show above the date. A few gown lines will show.

FINE
"IN GOD WE TRUST" will be complete but show weakness at the top. "LIBERTY" will also be complete although weak.

EXTREMELY FINE
All of the feathers will show but not distinctly.

ABOUT UNCIRCULATED
Only a trace of wear will show on the neck and the top outside edge of the right wing.

TRADE DOLLARS 1873-1885

GOOD
The motto "E PLURIBUS UNUM" above the eagle will be worn away.

VERY GOOD
A partial "E PLURIBUS UNUM" will show. About one-third of the feathers will be visible.

FINE
"E PLURIBUS UNUM" will show although a few letters will be weak. Half of the feathers will be visible.

VERY FINE

"IN GOD WE TRUST" and "LIBERTY" will be strong. The major details of the gown will be visible.

EXTREMELY FINE

All of the gown lines will show especially in Liberty's lap. There will be wear on the head, breast and left leg.

ABOUT UNCIRCULATED

Only a trace of wear will appear on Liberty's left knee, tip of her left breast and the hair above her ear.

GOLD DOLLARS 1849-1854 TYPE I

FINE

A full "LIBERTY" will be visible. The hair will be worn smooth all along the forehead and above the ear.

VERY FINE

The hair will be outlined above the forehead and around the neck.

VERY FINE

There will be a strong "E PLURIBUS UNUM" but it will show definite wear. Three-quarters of the feathers are now visible.

EXTREMELY FINE

All of the feathers will be visible. Wear will show on the head, knee and outer edges of the wings.

ABOUT UNCIRCULATED

Only a trace of wear will show on the head, knee and tops of the wings.

GOLD DOLLARS 1849-1854 TYPE I

FINE

The individual leaves will be well defined but fine details will not show.

VERY FINE

Some fine details will begin to show in the center of the leaves.

EXTREMELY FINE

All of the major hair detail will show. Wear will be visible on only the highest waves of hair.

ABOUT UNCIRCULATED

Only a trace of wear will appear on the tips of the curls above the forehead and ear.

Note: Gold coins are rarely found in conditions less than Fine.

GOLD DOLLARS 1854-1856 TYPE II

FINE

The hair will be worn smooth above the forehead and ear. Some of the feathers will be worn almost smooth.

VERY FINE

The hair will be outlined above the forehead and around the ear.

EXTREMELY FINE

All of the major hair detail will show.

Note: "LIBERTY" was often weakly struck on this series.

EXTREMELY FINE

All of the leaves will show fine center detail. Wear will be visible on the tips of the leaves.

ABOUT UNCIRCULATED

Only traces of wear will show on the tips of the leaves.

GOLD DOLLARS 1854-1856 TYPE II

FINE

The wreath will be boldly outlined but will show only major detail.

VERY FINE

Some of the fine leaf detail will begin to show.

EXTREMELY FINE

There will be wear on all the high points of the wreath.

ABOUT UNCIRCULATED

Just a trace of wear will show on the hair above the forehead.

GOLD DOLLARS 1856-1889 TYPE III

FINE

The hair above the forehead and ear will be worn smooth. The tops of the feathers will be smooth.

VERY FINE

The tops of the feathers and the hair around the face will be well outlined.

EXTREMELY FINE

All of the major hair detail will show. Only a slight amount of wear will be visible on the tips of the feathers.

ABOUT UNCIRCULATED

Only traces of wear will show on the tips of the feathers and on the hair above the ear and forehead.

ABOUT UNCIRCULATED

Only a trace of wear will appear on the tips of the leaves.

Note: The two center figures of the date often show severe weakness due to striking and should not affect the grade of the coin.

GOLD DOLLARS 1856-1889 TYPE III

FINE

The wreath will be boldly outlined but will show only major detail.

VERY FINE

Some of the fine leaf detail will begin to show.

EXTREMELY FINE

Wear will be visible on only the high points of the wreath.

ABOUT UNCIRCULATED

Just slight traces of wear will show on the tips of the leaves.

CAPPED QUARTER EAGLES 1796-1807

FINE

Liberty's cap will be worn almost smooth. Only the deepest waves of hair will show.

VERY FINE

The major detail of Liberty's cap will show. More hair detail will be visible.

Note: There may be weakness in the center of the obverse due to striking.

EXTREMELY FINE

There will be wear on the tops of the curls by Liberty's neck and on the highest folds of her cap.

ABOUT UNCIRCULATED

Only a trace of wear will be visible on the very top of the highest curls by Liberty's neck. A trace of wear will also be visible on the highest fold of her cap.

BUST QUARTER EAGLES 1808-1839

FINE

The hair above the forehead will be worn smooth. Only the deepest curls of the hair will show.

188

CAPPED QUARTER EAGLES 1796-1807

FINE

Only the deepest lines in the feathers will show. "E PLURIBUS UNUM" although readable will not be sharp.

VERY FINE

Most of the feathers will show but will be worn on the ends. "E PLURIBUS UNUM" will be sharp. The tail will show wear.

Note: "E PLURIBUS UNUM" may be weak in the center due to striking.

EXTREMELY FINE

Wear will be visible on the head, tail and the upper edges and tips of the wings.

ABOUT UNCIRCULATED

Only a trace of wear will show on the tip of the head and the extreme upper edges of the wings.

BUST QUARTER EAGLES 1808-1839

FINE

About half of the eagle's feathers will show. The neck will be worn smooth.

"LIBERTY" will be very bold. All of the major hair detail will show.

EXTREMELY FINE

Wear will be visible on the high points of the hair or cap above "LIBERTY" and on the curls around the neck.

ABOUT UNCIRCULATED

Only a trace of wear will show on the very highest tips of the hair and cap.

Note: The same hair rules for grading should be used for the three minor types in this series.

LIBERTY HEAD QUARTER EAGLES
1840-1907

FINE

"LIBERTY" will be complete but the "L" and "Y" may be weak. The hair curl on the neck although outlined will not show detail.

VERY FINE

"LIBERTY" will be bold. The major hair detail will show.

VERY FINE
Considerable wear will show on the head, neck and the edges and tips of the wings.

EXTREMELY FINE
Wear will be visible on the head, neck and the upper edges of the wings.

Note: Weakness due to striking may appear on the eagle's right wing.

ABOUT UNCIRCULATED
Only a trace of wear will appear on the highest point of the upper edges of the wings and the highest feathers on the neck.

LIBERTY HEAD QUARTER EAGLES
1840-1907

FINE
About half of the feathers will show on the wings. The neck will be worn almost smooth.

VERY FINE
Three-quarters of the feathers will show.

EXTREMELY FINE

Wear will appear on the tops of the waves of hair above the forehead and ear and on top of the head.

ABOUT UNCIRCULATED

There will be only a trace of wear on the hair above the ear and forehead.

INDIAN HEAD QUARTER EAGLES 1908-1929

VERY FINE

The design on the band just above the forehead will be well worn and show only partial detail.

EXTREMELY FINE

The design on the band just above the forehead will be complete. Wear will be visible on the cheek, the feathers behind the ear and the row of small feathers on top of the head.

ABOUT UNCIRCULATED

Only a trace of wear will show on the cheek. The small row of feathers will show wear on the tips.

EXTREMELY FINE

All of the feathers will show but there will be wear on the end of each feather.

ABOUT UNCIRCULATED

Only a trace of wear will be visible on the head just below the eagle's eye, the tips of the wings and on the eagle's left claw.

INDIAN HEAD QUARTER EAGLES 1908-1929

VERY FINE

The neck and upper end of the wing will be worn smooth. The feathers in the top half of the wing and the breast will show wear.

EXTREMELY FINE

Wear will show on the neck, breast and tip of the wing.

ABOUT UNCIRCULATED

Only a trace of wear will be visible on the upper neck and on the tops of the feathers at the tip of the wing.

THREE DOLLAR GOLD 1854-1889

FINE

The hair above the forehead will be worn into the bottom of the first few letters of "LIBERTY." The tops of the feathers will be worn smooth.

VERY FINE

The tops of the feathers will be well outlined but will show little detail. The hair above the forehead will touch "LI" of "LIBERTY."

EXTREMELY FINE

The hair above the forehead will be outlined but worn on the high point. All major details will show in the hair and on the feathers.

ABOUT UNCIRCULATED

A trace of wear will appear on the hair above the forehead and ear and on the tips of the feathers.

Note: The hair curls by the neck often come weakly struck and cannot be used to determine condition.

CAPPED HALF EAGLES 1795-1807

VERY FINE

The hair, cap and bust will show wear on the high points.

THREE DOLLAR GOLD 1854-1889

FINE

The wreath will be boldly outlined but show only major detail.

VERY FINE

Some of the fine leaf detail will begin to show.

EXTREMELY FINE

There will be wear on all the high points of the wreath.

ABOUT UNCIRCULATED

Only a trace of wear will show on the ends of the leaves and the ribbon knot.

Note: The date may be weak due to striking.

CAPPED HALF EAGLES 1795-1807

(For small eagle reverses see page 201)

VERY FINE

Most of the feathers will show although worn on the ends. The tail will show wear.

EXTREMELY FINE

Wear will be visible on the highest points of the cap, the hair above the forehead and to the left of the ear.

ABOUT UNCIRCULATED

Only traces of wear will show on the highest waves of hair above the forehead and behind the ear.

Note: The hair by the neck may be weakly struck.

BUST HALF EAGLES 1807-1838

VERY FINE

"LIBERTY" will be very bold. All major details of the hair will show.

EXTREMELY FINE

Wear will be visible on the high points of the hair or cap above "LIBERTY" and on the lower hair curls.

ABOUT UNCIRCULATED

Only a trace of wear will show on the very highest tips of the hair and cap.

Note: the same basic rules for grading should be used for the three minor types in this series.

EXTREMELY FINE
Wear will be visible on the head, tail and the upper edges and tips of the wings.

ABOUT UNCIRCULATED
Only a trace of wear will show on the extreme upper edges of the wings and the tip of the head.
Note: "E PLURIBUS UNUM" may be weak in the center due to striking.

BUST HALF EAGLES 1807-1838

VERY FINE
Considerable wear will show on the head, neck and ends of the wings.

EXTREMELY FINE
Wear will be visible on the head, neck and upper edges of the wings.

ABOUT UNCIRCULATED
Only a trace of wear will appear on the highest part of the upper edge of the wings and the highest feathers on the neck.

LIBERTY HEAD HALF EAGLES 1839-1908

FINE

"LIBERTY" will be complete although the "L" may be weak. The hair will show considerable wear.

VERY FINE

"LIBERTY" will be bold. The major hair detail will show.

EXTREMELY FINE

Wear will appear on the tops of the waves of hair above the ear and forehead and on top of the head.

ABOUT UNCIRCULATED

There will be only a trace of wear on the hair above the ear and forehead.

INDIAN HEAD HALF EAGLES 1908-1929

VERY FINE

The design on the band just above the forehead will be well worn and show only partial detail.

LIBERTY HEAD HALF EAGLES 1839-1908

FINE

About half of the feathers will show on the wings. The neck will be worn almost smooth.

VERY FINE

Three-quarters of the feathers will show. More detail will appear on the eagle's right leg.

EXTREMELY FINE

All of the feathers will show but there will be wear on the end of each feather.

ABOUT UNCIRCULATED

Only a trace of wear will be visible on the head just below the eagle's eye, the tips of the wings and on the eagle's left claw.

INDIAN HEAD HALF EAGLES 1908-1929

VERY FINE

The neck and upper end of the wing will be worn smooth. The feathers in the top half of the wing and the breast will show wear.

EXTREMELY FINE

The design on the band just above the forehead will be complete. Wear will be visible on the cheek, the feathers behind the ear and the row of small feathers on top of the head.

ABOUT UNCIRCULATED

Only a trace of wear will show on the cheek. The small row of feathers will show wear on their tips.

CAPPED EAGLES 1795-1804

VERY FINE

The hair, cap and bust will show wear on the high points.

EXTREMELY FINE

Wear will be visible on the highest points of the cap, the hair above the forehead and to the left of the ear.

ABOUT UNCIRCULATED

Only traces of wear will show on the highest waves of hair above the forehead and behind the ear.

Note: The hair by the neck may be weakly struck.

200

EXTREMELY FINE
Wear will show on the neck, breast and tip of the wing.

ABOUT UNCIRCULATED
Only a trace of wear will be visible on the upper neck and on the tops of the feathers at the tip of the wing.

CAPPED EAGLES
1795-1804

VERY FINE
Most feathers will show but will be worn on the ends.

EXTREMELY FINE
Wear on head, breast and upper edges and tips of wings.

ABOUT UNCIRCULATED
Traces of wear on extreme edges of wings, tip of head and breast.

LIBERTY HEAD EAGLES 1838-1907

FINE
"LIBERTY" will be complete but the "L" may be weak. The hair will show considerable wear.

VERY FINE
"LIBERTY" will be bold. The major hair detail will show.

EXTREMELY FINE
Wear will appear on the top of the waves of hair above the forehead and ear and on top of the head.

ABOUT UNCIRCULATED
There will be only a trace of wear on the hair above the ear and forehead.

INDIAN HEAD EAGLES 1907-1933

VERY FINE
Considerable wear will show on the feathers just above the word "LIBERTY" and on the hair above the ear and forehead.

LIBERTY HEAD EAGLES 1838-1907

FINE
About half of the feathers will show on the wings. The neck will be worn almost smooth.

VERY FINE
About three-quarters of the feathers will show.

EXTREMELY FINE
All of the feathers will show but there will be wear on the end of each feather.

ABOUT UNCIRCULATED
Only a trace of wear will be visible on the head just below the eagle's eye and on the tips and extreme upper edges of the wings.

INDIAN HEAD EAGLES 1907-1933

VERY FINE
Approximately three-quarters of the eagle's feathers will show. Wear will be visible on the head, top of the left wing and high points of the legs.

EXTREMELY FINE

Slight wear will show on the hair and on the feathers just above the word "LIBERTY."

ABOUT UNCIRCULATED

There will be a trace of wear on the highest waves of hair above the ear and eye.

LIBERTY HEAD DOUBLE EAGLES 1849-1907

FINE

The hair on top of the head and below the coronet will be worn smooth. The curls by the neck will show only major details.

VERY FINE

The major hair detail will show on top of the head and below the coronet.

EXTREMELY FINE

Wear will show on the curls by the neck, hair above the ear and below the coronet.

EXTREMELY FINE

Less wear will show on the left wing, head and legs.

ABOUT UNCIRCULATED

Only a trace of wear will be visible on the tip of the left wing and tip of the head.

LIBERTY HEAD DOUBLE EAGLES 1849-1907

FINE

The eagle's head will be worn smooth. The tail and the tops of the wings will show considerable wear.

VERY FINE

All of the feathers will show on the wings but they will not be sharply detailed.

EXTREMELY FINE

The feathers on the wings will be sharp. Wear will be visible on the head, neck, tail and the highest points of the shield.

205

Only a trace of wear will be visible on the highest waves of hair.

Note: The hair curl directly under the ear will sometimes be weak due to striking.

ST. GAUDENS DOUBLE EAGLES 1907-1933

FINE

Liberty's right leg will be worn almost smooth. The gown line across the chest will be weak.

VERY FINE

More detail will be visible in Liberty's gown around the breasts and her lower right leg.

EXTREMELY FINE

There will be wear on the breasts and both knees.

ABOUT UNCIRCULATED

Only a trace of wear will show on the tips of the breasts and Liberty's left knee.

Note: A flat knee (not rubbed) and/or nose may appear on uncirculated coins due to stacking of the coins by the mint or banks.

206

ABOUT UNCIRCULATED

The slightest trace of wear will show on the eagle's neck and the top of the tail.

Note: "E PLURIBUS UNUM" will not always be fully readable even on uncirculated coins due to striking.

ST. GAUDENS DOUBLE EAGLES
1907-1933

FINE

The forward edge of the left wing will show wear. The breast and leg will show smooth spots of wear.

VERY FINE

Just the tip of the left wing will show wear. The breast will show a smooth spot of wear. Wear will be visible on the leg but the feathers will be discernible.

EXTREMELY FINE

All of the feathers will show except a small spot on the breast just behind the neck.

ABOUT UNCIRCULATED

The slightest trace of wear will be noticeable on the breast just behind the neck.

Note: Heavy bag marks will lower the value of scarcer pieces.

INDEX